D0456942

# EveryDay Professional Writing

# EveryDay
# Professional
# Writing

—◆—

*Laurie Rozakis, Ph.D.*

MADISON
PARK
PRESS™

NEW YORK

Published by Madison Park Press, One Penn Plaza, New York, NY 10119. Madison Park Press is a trademark of Bertelsmann Direct North America, Inc.

Book design by Christos Peterson

ISBN: 978-1-58288-295-6

Printed in the United States of America

# CONTENTS

———◆———

# EveryDay
# Professional
# Writing

# CHAPTER 1

## Discover a Different Kind of Writing

---

**YOU MUST REMEMBER THIS**
Professional writing is the process of generating or gathering information and presenting it to an audience in a clear, logical, and easily understandable form.

**ALL THE RIGHT MOVES**
Modern life demands that you produce professional documents, no matter what your job, career, or situation.

According to a popular urban legend, a monkey hitting keys at random on a typewriter would eventually type the complete works of William Shakespeare. It's an intriguing idea, but totally nonsensical, unfortunately for the ambitious monkeys of the world. That's because writing is a uniquely human activity. Animals can't write, no matter how long we leave them at a keyboard and how many treats we give them. But humans *can* write, and they can write in a dazzling array of styles—even without the benefit of time and treats.

We can write fiction: novels, screenplays, and short stories. We can write nonfiction, too, including autobiographies, articles, biographies, blogs, creative nonfiction, e-mail, essays, journals, legal briefs, letters, literary criticism, newspaper and magazine articles, and postcards. We can write slogans and signs, drama and poetry. We call some of these prodigious literary accomplishments "creative writing." We call other of these creations "professional writing." What's the difference? What is professional writing, anyway?

## How Much Do You Know About Professional Writing?

Mark each of these statements as true or false.

_____ 1. All professional writing is done in a workplace setting, such as a business, a school, or a company.

_____ 2. You can produce professional writing from a cruise ship, a space ship, a battleship—from anywhere. You can turn out professional writing from your home, too.

_____ 3. You can't produce any professional writing unless you have a real job.

_____ 4. Anyone can write professional documents, whether employed or not.

_____ 5. Few people will ever have to produce any professional writing.

_____ 6. Everyone will have to produce some professional writing, no matter who they are or what they do.

_____ 7. We can hire professional writers easily. There are people who do this type of writing for us.

_____ 8. Hiring people to produce professional writing isn't easy at all, because few people write clearly and concisely.

_____ 9. There is basically only one kind of professional writing.

_____ 10. There are many different kinds of professional writing.

_____ 11. Being able to produce professional writing is an inborn skill. This kind of writing cannot be taught or learned. Either you have it or you don't.

_____ 12. With the appropriate guidance and training, anyone can learn to create effective, powerful professional documents. Writing is a skill and, like any other skill, can be taught and learned. You just need a desire to learn and an ability to stick to a task.

*Answers*

All the odd-numbered items are false. All the even-numbered items are true.

> Professional writers can have a variety of job titles, such as *writer, editor, Web designer, information developer*, and *documentation specialist*, depending on the media in which they write.

## What Is Professional Writing?

*Professional writing* is the process of generating or gathering information from experts and presenting it to an audience in a clear, logical, and easily understandable form. Professional writers gather knowledge from experts by conducting interviews and reading previously published material. The writer then studies the audience and determines the best way to present the information. Should it be a Web site? A book? A brochure? An illustration? A chart? The writer reshapes the information so that the audience can easily understand it and act upon it.

## How Professional Writing Is Used

Professional writing has other uses as well. Often, a skilled professional writer refashions highly technical material from scientists and other experts so that laypeople can understand it. Professional writers thus serve almost as "translators" between technical people and everyday people, sharing vital knowledge and information in such fields as medicine (new drugs), economics (stock and bond trends), and meteorology (hurricanes and earthquakes). Professional writers work with engineers, managers, policy makers; in short, with experts of every stripe.

Some people trained as professional writers go on to careers in the professions themselves, earning graduate degrees as scientists (PhD's), doctors (MDs), and fund managers (MBAs, CFAs). Others work as professional writers at newspapers, magazines, think tanks, and businesses. Here are some areas where professional writers typically hold jobs:

| | |
|---|---|
| Accounting | Law |
| Bilingual communication | Library science |
| Consulting | Marketing |
| Economics | Medicine |
| Editing documents | Museums |
| Education | Public policy |
| Engineering | Public relations |
| Government positions | Publishing |
| Human resources | Scientific fields |
| Intercultural communication | Stock market careers |
| Information design | Technical writing |
| Journalism | Web site content |

In these positions, professional writers produce a wide variety of writing, including articles of all sorts, brochures, educational texts, environmental impact statements, grant proposals, newsletters, online information, pamphlets, press releases, public interest material, scientific pieces, and textbooks.

Here are additional examples of professional writing:

Case studies
Corporate annual reports
Design specifications
Disaster-preparedness
manuals
Film scripts
Homeland Security planning
Manuals
Network administrators'
guides
Online FAQs and help
guides
Presentations
Proposals
Site preparation guides
Test reports
Troubleshooting guides
Tutorials
White papers

## How You Can Use Professional Writing Skills

You may want to have a career as a professional writer. However, most people just want to beef up their writing skills so they can become more skilled at producing professionally written documents in their private lives as well as in their careers. These documents include résumés and cover letters, for instance. We all want to write with a clear, crisp style on the job and at home. We all want to write more easily, quickly, and painlessly, too.

## You've Got the Goods!

You've bought this book and you're reading it, which shows that you want to become more skilled at professional writing. What skills have you brought to the table? Overall, effective professional writers have the following qualities. Check the ones that apply to you.

In general, professional writers are
_____ creative
_____ self-starters
_____ curious about the world around them

_____ comfortable working with others

_____ secure on their own as well

_____ independent thinkers

_____ interested in innovations in print and digital media

_____ skilled with grammar, usage, and mechanics—and ways to find the answers to the questions they don't know

_____ knowledgeable about design elements and their importance

_____ familiar with templates or willing to learn about them

As global economies become increasingly interconnected thanks to digital media, we've seen a sharply increased demand for professional writers in business, industry, government, education, health care, and nonprofit organizations. But we've seen an equally great need for people to write professionally in their everyday lives, especially in community groups such as the Parent-Teacher Association, library boards, school boards, and other citizens' groups. These grassroots groups have become very important places to effect significant social change.

## Technical Writing Versus School Writing

As my college students have discovered to their astonishment, professional writing is *very* different from school writing. In the chapters that follow, I'll cover each and every difference in detail, but to make sure that we're all on the same page from the very start, I'd like to share some examples of professional and school writing with you. As you compare and contrast them, pay close attention to the format, words, tone, and audience.

### Design Elements

In general, professional writing is highly designed to make it easier to read. Professional writing often uses bullets, numbered lists, illustrations, charts, graphs, and other visual aids. School writing rarely, if ever, has these elements. Rather, school writing is simply paragraphs of text. They are likely indented, but no additional formatting is added.

### Language and Tone

Further, professional writing usually has a neutral tone, formal language, and lack of an individual voice. School writing, in contrast, emphasizes an individual voice and different levels of diction, from casual to formal.

> **Voice** is the writer's personality, expressed through word choice, sentence length and variety, figures of speech, tone, and punctuation. It is the sense that a distinct person with a distinct personality is speaking through the words.

### Point of View

School writing is often in the first-person, especially when it comes to essays; professional writing is more often in the third-person. As a result, school writing usually conveys the writer's personality, while professional writing conveys a business-like demeanor.

### Purpose

Last, but certainly not least, professional writing usually explains (exposition), persuades, (persuasion), or describes (description). School writing can have all of those three purposes, but it can also tell a story (narrate), and often does.

## Memos

A *memo* (short for "memorandum") is a document typically used for communication within a company. Memos can be as formal as a business letter or a report preface. However, the heading and overall tone make a memo different from a business letter. Because you generally send memos to coworkers and colleagues, you don't have to include a formal salutation or closing remark. Here's a sample:

---

To All . . .

When students need to have their e-mail/wireless passwords changed, they will now be reset back to their default (mmddyyssss—birth date followed by the last 4 digits of their social security number).

For those students who need to have their passwords changed, please e-mail me the following information: first and last name, user name, and the last 4 digits of their social security number.

Thanks.

---

## Instructions

*Instructions* are explanations of a process, method, task, or other job. The steps are presented as commands, written in chronological (time) order, and often numbered or bulleted. Here is an example:

---

How to Care for Your New Carpet

Simple everyday upkeep will help maintain the beauty of your new carpet. One important aspect of this care is cleaning up food and beverage spills quickly and correctly. Follow these steps:

1. Blot up as much of the spill as possible. Use a clean, white cloth or white paper towels.
2. Press down firmly to remove as much liquid as you can. Do not rub the stain, because rubbing can change the texture of the carpet. Continue blotting with clean cloths or paper towels until the stain is gone.

3. If the stain does not disappear, mix 1 quart warm water with 1 tea-spoon mild liquid laundry detergent. Cover the stain with the clean-er. Let it sit five minutes. Then blot up the liquid with clean white cloths or paper towels.
4. Rinse the stained area with warm water and blot until the carpet is almost dry.
5. When the carpet is completely dry, vacuum it. To restore the tex-ture, you may then wish to brush the carpet gently.

If you need additional assistance, call 800-555-CLEAN.

In chapter 6, you'll learn all about how to write clear, use-ful instructions.

## Letters

A *letter* is a written communication from one person or entity to another. Letters fall into two broad categories: friendly let-ters and professional letters.

- *Friendly letters* send personal wishes, update friends on news, share views, and convey thanks, sympathy, love, and other important emotions.

- *Professional letters*, in contrast, conduct business. For instance, a professional letter would thank a per-son for an interview with the purpose of furthering the writer's chances of securing the job.

As a result, friendly letters can be keyboarded, but they are often handwritten; professional letters, in contrast, are always keyboarded.

Here is an example:

---

Dear Mrs. Rozakis,

I heard about the presentation you did for Farmingdale in reference to on-line communities. I belong to the organization LICSPA (Long Island Council of Student Personnel Administrators) and every month we gather and discuss issues facing us in Higher Education. Our topic for December is On-line Communities/Chat Rooms. I wanted to know if you would like to present this topic to our group.

The meeting is scheduled for Friday, December 14th, at Dowling College.

Please feel free to check out our Web site at *www.licspa.net* to learn more about the organization.

If you can let me know that you are available by Monday, November 5th, that would be great.

Thank you,

Jennifer Petterson
LICSPA Secretary

Student Center
Hudson University
Anyplace, USA

---

In chapter 7, you'll learn all about how to write powerful professional letters.


## Résumés

A résumé is a list of your relevant job experience, education, and personal information. As with much of professional writing, a résumé is highly formatted with a very specific format. In this instance, the format depends on the method of transmission (via U.S. mail, e-mail, or fax, for instance) as much as on convention. Here is an example of a résumé:

---

# LING LI

12345 MAIN STREET • HAMPTON, SC 12789
PHONE (555) 456-7890 • FAX (123) 098-7654
LING-LI@GMAIL.COM

## OBJECTIVE

To gain full-time employment as a purchasing director

## EXPERIENCE

1999–present        Vincent's, Inc.                Southridge, SC
*Purchasing Agent*
- Negotiate with vendors to save $3 million yearly as a result of corporate rebate programs, maximum discounts, and rapid payment discounts.
- Maintain and upgrade all equipment as necessary, saving $100,000 in leasing costs per year.
- Train and supervise staff on procedure and daily assignments.
- Estimate pre-construction costs for equipment based on design drawings.

1997–1999     Vincent's, Inc                Winterville, SC
*Office Services Manager*
- Negotiated and ordered all office supplies and business machines.
- Implemented training course for new recruits, speeding profitability.
- Distributed biweekly payroll packages to 650 company restaurants.

1990–1997     Caron's Good Eats                Brookhaven, SC
*Purchasing Assistant*
- Negotiated bids with trucking services and scheduled deliveries.

---

- Secured warehouse space for equipment storage, saving $150,000 yearly.
- Tracked orders to ensure timely delivery, resulting in 35 percent greater on-time rate.

### EDUCATION

| | | |
|---|---|---|
| 2002–2006 | Lincoln University | Newton, NC |

- B.A., Business Administration.
- Graduated Summa Cum Laude.

### SKILLS

Excellent oral and written communication skills. Proficient in AS400 computer system regarding purchasing, payroll, and accounting. Knowledge of various computer programs, including Microsoft Word and Excel for Windows.

In chapter 8, you'll learn how to write powerful, effective résumés that will help you get jobs.

## Proposals

A *proposal* is an offering from a seller to a prospective buyer. Proposals can range in size from a one-page letter to several hundred pages of detailed specifications. Proposals are common in academia as well as in business.

Here's a proposal that I wrote. It was accepted and funded.

### Application for Special Projects Fund Support

| | |
|---|---|
| From: | Professor Laurie Rozakis |
| To: | State of New York/United University Professions Joint Labor Management Committees |
| Date: | January 5, 2007; revised March 2007 |

Fact:   A study released by the U.S. Education Department provides new evidence that colleges are reducing the percentage of full-time positions on their faculties.

*The study found that from 1993 to 1998, 40 percent of all institutions took action to reduce the size of their full-time faculties. Almost a quarter of those institutions did so by replacing full-time faculty members with part-time faculty members.*

(Source: "Colleges Have Cut Proportion of Full-Time Faculty Members, Study Finds," by Piper Fogg. *The Chronicle of Higher Education*, 11-02-2001)

Fact:   According to the American Federation of Teachers, from 1971 to 1986, the number of part-time faculty at U.S. colleges and universities increased by 133 percent, while full-time faculty increased 22 percent.

(Source: 1996 American Federation of Teachers Statement on Part-Time Faculty Employment).

Fact:   An article in *Newsday* reports that *Farmingdale State President Jonathan Gibralter said increasing enrollment has placed more demands on its $29.4 million budget . . . He said the college has not had to make program cuts, but staffing needs are acute. "I lost 12 full-time faculty to early retirement," he said, "and 35 faculty and staff overall." He's had to hire more adjuncts to take up the slack in the classroom, a $1 million expenditure, he said.*

(Source: "Waiting for the Ax: LI College Administrators Know More Budget Cuts May Come" by Olivia Winslow. *Newsday*. 9-02-03)

According to the Farmingdale State Web page (Farmingdale.edu), "At Farmingdale, we offer you small, personalized classes with a dedicated faculty. We believe that the relationships formed between you and your professors assure you of the individual attention that enables your success. **Our faculty is comprised of over 170 full-time profes-**

**sors and 120 adjunct faculty members** ready to help you to grow academically and personally. . . ."

Fact:   When I started at Farmingdale State nearly 20 years ago, we had 36 full-time teachers in the English department and fewer than 10 adjuncts. Today, we have 8 full-time teachers and more than 40 adjuncts.

Fact:   We are not doing all we can to integrate adjuncts into our community and help them be as effective as they can be.

When I realized this situation two years ago, I came up with the idea of making packets to distribute to our adjuncts. Working with my chair, I wrote a letter outlining the adjuncts' responsibilities. The enclosed letter briefly describes the adjunct's responsibilities, explains our payment schedule, outlines the parking policy, and provides information on related "housekeeping" issues such as keys, mailbox, observations, and school closings. I added a campus map and some chalk and packed the whole thing in a manila envelope. I did this on my own time and it took several months to coordinate efforts.

Now, I request $1,000 to expand these fledgling efforts into an orientation booklet for *all* adjuncts at Farmingdale State. This would be an easy-to-use, practical guide for all adjuncts in all departments. **The $1,000 would help cover the printing costs.**

Farmingdale has a professional handbook (revised 2003) for full-time faculty. There is no such handbook across the university for adjuncts, although two schools have small pamphlets. I am deeply indebted to Dental Hygiene and the Computer Systems Department for these pamphlets and the valuable information they provide.

**The Booklet**

I have a proven track record in this field, having published more than 100 books with major trade publishers (including The Literary Guild,

Scholastic, McGraw-Hill, and Penguin Putnam). Please see the attached C.V.

My proposed handbook would contain input from **all** departments and contain some or all of the following headings. *This list is tentative, pending input from all departments, the administration, the academic administration, United University Professions, and Human Resources:*

Before Classes Begin:
During the Semester:
At the End of the Semester:
General Information:

The booklet will be reviewed and updated on a regular basis. The tentative schedule is every three years.

**I believe that such a booklet is indispensable to attracting and keeping dedicated teachers.**

Thank you for considering my proposal. A special thank you to the Computer Systems Department for their invaluable suggestions.

## E-mail

*E-mail* is an abbreviation for electronic mail, a way to write, store, send, and receive messages over computers. E-mail is the most common form of written communication in the world today.

In chapter 10, you'll learn how to write professional e-mail.

## Web Pages

Professional writers often design and create Web pages, too. The Web pages can be used for businesses, organizations, the government, the military, schools, and private individuals. Web pages are becoming one the most significant forms of written communication in the twenty-first century.

Whether you have to write a lot for your job or a little, you know that learning about professional writing can help in all your various careers: worker, parent, or community member.

# CHAPTER 2

## Explore Audience and Purpose

---

**YOU MUST REMEMBER THIS**
**Audience** is made up of the people who will read your writing.
**Purpose** is the reason why you are writing: to explain, to persuade, and/or to describe.

**ALL THE RIGHT MOVES**
Consider your audience and purpose every time you write a single word for a professional document. Make sure that you have pinpointed each one.

---

You learned in chapter 1 that professional writing differs significantly from school and personal writing in many ways. Nonetheless, all writing is the same in one crucial way: it can be difficult figuring out what to say. Not to worry: you'll get all the help you need in this chapter.

Getting started writing all professional documents is much easier when you focus on the following two elements: audience and purpose. These elements are critical when it comes to writing powerful and effective professional documents. Knowing them contributes mightily to an easier process and a better product, so let's get started.

## Audience: Your Readers

What is the very first step you take when you begin to write a professional document? Check the step you would complete first:

\_\_\_\_\_ decide which topic to choose
\_\_\_\_\_ find out if you are writing alone or as part of a group
\_\_\_\_\_ gather the facts you need from online and print sources
\_\_\_\_\_ interview people who know a lot about your topic
\_\_\_\_\_ create a time line to allocate each part of the assignment
\_\_\_\_\_ identify and assess your audience

While there's no doubt that all six steps are important every time you write any professional document, the most important point is the last one—*identify and assess your audience.* Your audience is comprised of the person or people who will read your writing.

Even before you focus on a topic, it's critical that you identify your audience. That's because every audience brings its own set of preconceived notions to your document. You can never meet your readers' needs if you don't know who they are and what they think about you, your company, your product, and your message. To write successful professional documents, you must adjust your message to meet the needs of your audience.

### A Wide Range of Readers

Here are some possible audiences for your documents:

| | |
|---|---|
| clients and potential clients | relatives |
| colleagues | strangers |
| community members | subordinates |
| superiors | superiors |
| friends | teachers |
| neighbors | |

Your audience can be made up of people who are young or old or somewhere in between. They might be male or female, Republicans or Democrats, Americans or foreigners. They can be rich or poor, professionals or worker bees. They can be highly knowledgeable about your topic or totally ignorant of it.

One of the things that makes professional writing challenging is that you may not know your audience. After all, when you speak to someone in person, you know exactly to whom you are speaking. But when you're writing, you don't always know exactly who will read your document.

Audiences for professional writing can be divided into three broad categories:

1. *Lay audience:* These readers have an everyday knowledge of your topic. They are likely to be very knowledgeable about their own work, but not about yours. As a result, they will require some additional detail and background information to understand the technical aspects of your document. With this audience, visuals such as charts, diagrams, graphs, and photographs are especially helpful.

2. *Administrative audience:* These readers do know about your topic, but they are not as proficient as you are because they have not studied the topic in the depth that you have. After all, that's why they hired you to write the document in the first place! For this audience, be sure to include facts, details, examples, visuals, and any other information they'll need to help them make informed decisions.

3. *Expert audience:* These readers know a lot about the topic, so they rarely have to be filled in on the details, as the other two audiences do. They likely have advanced degrees in the area of study you are writing about and many years working in the field. However, since they are so proficient in the topic, they require jargon (the specialized vocabulary in

the field) and proof of your assertions, which is likely to take the form of respected, timely research studies.

Further, you are likely to have both a primary audience and a secondary audience.

- Your *primary audience* is comprised of the people you send the message to.

- Your *secondary audience* is comprised of other people who read your message.

For instance, let's say that you send a proposal to your boss for a new business plan. Your boss is so pleased with your plan that she brings it to a group meeting and shares it with her colleagues and people a bit higher on the corporate food chain. Your primary audience was your boss because you intended the document for her eyes only. Your secondary audience has become everyone else who will read the memo, people you did not have in mind when you wrote it.

### *How to Get a Handle on Your Audience*

There's no magic to analyzing your audience: it's just plain old investigation. Try the following techniques:

1. *Interview the people who will read your documents to discover what they know.* Ask them questions designed to elicit their level of knowledge.

2. *Speak to colleagues and managers who have already written for people in this particular audience.* Find out what information they included . . . and what information they omitted.

3. *Read trade journals and research in the field.* This is an excellent way to gauge your audience's level of knowledge.

4. *Use surveys.* Ask potential audience members questions such as these:"What do you need to know from my document? What information can I provide to you? What is your reason for reading this document?"

5. *Attend trade conferences.* Speak to exhibitors and visitors, read the literature offered, and assess people's level of knowledge about your topic. See what information they need and want.

6. *Run a focus group.* People in advertising, marketing, and publishing rely on this technique. They gather a representative sampling of the audience and have them examine the document in its draft stages.

Pay close attention to your audience's *bias*, their preconceived notions. Every person has bias, which is fine—as long as you recognize it and deal with it. Determine whether your readers have strong opinions about your topic and the information you intend to present. If they have already formed strong opinions or even reached a conclusion contrary to your own, you must formulate an approach to change their minds. Perhaps you'll present a lot of detail, such as facts, statistics, or examples. You might appeal to emotion as well as reason, for instance.

*Different Audiences = Different Needs*

Knowing your audience helps you make critical decisions about your style so you can meet your readers' specific needs. For instance, say you have to write two documents about the safety of nuclear reactors. The first document is for a seminar of nuclear physicists; the second, for a third-grade science textbook. You would use a great deal of technical jargon and complex ideas for the nuclear physicists, but you would use simple words and concepts for the children. Then your writing is meeting the needs of each group. Thus, consider your audience's *frame of reference*—what they know and where they are coming from as they approach your topic.

The following chart shows some of the decisions you must make on the basis of your audience:

| Consideration | Choices |
|---|---|
| Words | Everyday or technical? Easy or difficult? Long or short? |
| Sentences | Long or short? Simple or complex? |
| Tone | Formal or informal? Serious or more light-hearted? |
| Details | Specialized or general? A lot of detail or a little? |
| Topic | Technical or general? Common or uncommon? |
| Visuals | Charts? Graphs? Line drawings? Photographs? Flow charts? Web support? Color or black and white? |
| Margins | Standard or not? One column, two columns, or some other arrangement? |
| Font choice | Traditional or contemporary? Serif or sans serif? |
| Font size | Large or small? 8 point? 10 point? 11 point? 12 point? 13 point? Or some other choice? |
| Attitude | Friendly or hostile? Neutral? |

We'll explore these elements further in chapter 3.

## FONT TYPES

*Serif type* has extensions on some letters, as you can see on these examples: T, N, H.

*Sans serif type* does not have the extensions, as you can see on these letters: T, N, H.

Serifs matter because they affect how readable a font is and how your audience perceives it. A serif type such as Times New Roman is usually perceived (often unconsciously) as traditional, stately, and trustworthy. A sans serif font such as Arial is often perceived as modern, clean, and fresh.

Always try to visualize your audience as you write, as this will make it much easier for you to meet its needs.

### Use a Checklist

Use a checklist such as the following one as you decide what information to present and how to present it:

1. *Include what your audience needs.*
   Make sure that you have included critical details. This is especially important if you have a wide, general audience. Novices, for instance, often need a lot more details than more experienced, expert readers.

2. *Omit what your audience doesn't need.*
   This sounds like common sense, and it is. Nonetheless, many writers find it difficult to omit information even if they know it's not needed. After all, they've worked hard crafting those words and they don't want to cut so much as a single one. However, unnecessary information tends to confuse readers and lead them astray from your main point. Forewarned is forearmed, so you won't be like this!

3. *Include concrete examples.*
   The more specific your examples, the more effective they will be. Examples are especially useful to clarify difficult and abstract text aimed at a lay audience.

4. *Use ample visuals.*
   Writers used to an academic setting may be unwilling to include pictures, thinking they're too elementary.

Remember: One picture is worth a thousand words. Further, not everyone learns best by reading words. Many people process information more quickly by looking at visuals such as diagrams and flow charts, so don't be afraid to include ample visuals.

5. *Use the most appropriate method of organization.*
Information can be organized in many ways, so choose the method that best suits your audience and topic. For instance, professional documents that give directions or instructions are usually arranged in time order, the steps presented from first to last. Here are some other ways to arrange your material:

- Order of space (top to bottom, bottom to top, inside out, outside in, etc.)

- Order of time (first to last, last to first, etc.)

- Order of importance (most to least important, least to most important, etc.)

- Advantages and disadvantages

- Cause and effect

6. *Link related ideas with transitions.*
Transitions help readers follow your ideas. The following chart shows some of the most common transitions and the relationships they express:

| Relationship | Transitions |
|---|---|
| addition | and again, and then, besides, equally important, finally, further, furthermore, nor, too, next, last, what's more, moreover, in addition, first (second, etc.) |
| comparison | whereas, but, yet, on the other hand, however, nevertheless, on the contrary, by comparison, where, compared to, up against, balanced against, vis-à-vis, although, conversely, meanwhile, after all, in contrast, although this may be true |
| repetition, emphasis | in brief, as I have said, as I have noted, as has been noted, yet, still, however, nevertheless, in spite of, despite, of course, once in a while, sometimes, definitely, extremely, obviously, in fact, indeed, in any case, absolutely, positively, naturally, surprisingly, always, forever, never, emphatically, unquestionably, without a doubt, certainly, undeniably, without reservation |
| time order | a, b, c, etc. <br> 1, 2, 3, etc. <br> after, after a few hours, afterward, and so forth, at this time, at this point, before this, concurrently, consequently, finally, first, following this, formerly, hence, immediately, later, next, now, previously, second, simultaneously, soon, subsequently, then, thereafter, therefore, third, thus |
| examples | to give an example, for example, for instance, in this case, in another case, on this occasion, in this situation, take the case of, to demonstrate, to illustrate, as an illustration |

7. *Write shorter chunks of text.*

In academic essays and compositions, we're used to writing long paragraphs. In professional writing, however, shorter blocks of text are almost always easier for your audience to grasp and process. This is especially important when it comes to writing e-mail, as you'll learn in chapter 10.

8. *Write clear introductions.*

You know that first impressions matter a lot when you're meeting someone. They matter a lot when you're writing, too. Get started on the right foot with your writing and your audience will understand your message, be able to follow the steps in your instructions, be more likely to agree with your opinion, and more clearly visualize what you are describing.

9. *Use "you."*

Every time you write, you make a series of choices. For instance, you choose the point of view that you want to use. This is the vantage point from which you present your material. Here are your choices: first-person, second-person, or third-person point of view. We use different personal pronouns to indicate the point of view. The following chart shows the choices you have:

| Personal Pronouns | | | |
|---|---|---|---|
| **Pronouns** | **Nominative Case** | **Objective Case** | **Possessive Case** |
| first person | I, we | me, us | my, mine, our, ours |
| second person | you | you | your, yours |
| third person | he, she, it, they | him, her, it, them | his, her, hers, it, their, theirs |

In school writing, you rarely use the second person, "you." In professional writing, however, you'll often use "you" to address your audience directly. Using "you" helps you:

- Write simply and directly

- Link to your readers

- Establish a natural, comfortable tone

As a general rule, avoid the second-person "you" in very formal documents such as scholarship and legal papers.

10. *Use headings and subheadings.*
    These textural features make it a lot easier for your audience to follow your ideas. It is a basic consideration: headings and subheadings give your readers guideposts to follow.

## Purpose

*Purpose* is your reason for writing. Every professional document has a purpose. The three main purposes are: *exposition, persuasion,* and *description*.

### Exposition
This is writing that explains, shows, or tells. This type of writing is found in school writing as well as professional writing.

### Persuasion
This is writing that attempts to convince someone through reasons, examples, statistics, ethics, and/or emotion. As with expo-

sition, this type of writing is common in school writing as well as professional writing.

### Description

This is writing that uses the five senses to paint a word picture of a person, place, or thing. This type of writing is more common in school writing than in professional writing, although it is a component of all professional writing, as you must describe something to explain or persuade.

The following chart shows the purpose of some common professional documents. You'll notice that some types of professional writing can fulfill more than one purpose, depending on how they are used.

| Purpose | Examples |
| --- | --- |
| Exposition | abstracts, business plans, case studies, disaster preparedness manuals, e-mails, instructions, letters, memos, network administrators' guides, online FAQs and help guides, organizational policies, press releases, progress reports, proposals, scientific reports, textbooks, troubleshooting guides, user guides, white papers, wills |
| Persuasion | appeals for funds, corporate annual reports, cover letters, e-mails, job evaluations, letters, memos, proposals, recommendations, reports, résumés |
| Description | e-mails, letters, memos, reports |

# CHAPTER 3

## Master Design Elements

---

**YOU MUST REMEMBER THIS**
Professional writing uses design elements such as margins, fonts, white space, boxes, bullets, and color to help readers understand your message better.

**ALL THE RIGHT MOVES**
Plan your documents from the very beginning, choose a design that suits your message, and keep it simple. Highlight the main points, be consistent with your use of design features, and make the design clear to your reader so it is easy to follow.

Professional writing is not merely compiling information on a topic. If it were, I wouldn't have to write this book! Rather, professional writing involves making a series of very conscious choices. You learned in chapter 2 that two of the most important choices are your audience and your purpose. Other critical decisions involve how you will present your information.

We judge people on their appearance. Oh, we may deny it (as in "it's what's inside that counts"), but we all know that what's outside counts as well. In the same way, we judge a professional document by its appearance. But when it comes to professional writing, appearance takes on greater urgency than mere vanity because the way the material is presented in a document can help or hinder how well you convey your message to your audience. It even affects whether your message is read and if so, whether or not it is read thoroughly. Let me prove it to you now.

## Test Case

What's the difference between these two documents?

Document #1:

My name is Argie Ruiz. I live at 17 West Main Street, Apt. 4B, Salt Lake City, UT 84101. My phone number is 801-555-5555. My e-mail is argieruiz@gmail.com. I am an accomplished editorial manager with more than ten years of experience in editing, writing, and education. I have developed instructional, basal, and supplementary materials, formative assessments, and state-specific alignments in reading, language arts, mathematics, and science, K–12.

My current job is at the Leading Learning Edge in Salt Lake City, UT. I started there in 2002 as a senior editor. I worked in the assessment group. Now I manage a new group developing state-specific materials for all content areas, as well as all national assessment components and state customizations for a new reading program. My duties include product development, marketing, and working with ad hoc groups and focus test groups. I also hire and train staff, oversee editorial process, and produce market-driven products.

I am responsible for research, product development, and management of all national and state-specific reading assessments, K–6, in compliance with NCLB, including screening, diagnostic, progress monitoring tools, formative and summative assessments, fluency, and running record materials. I have initiated a successful corporate partnership with an early reading assessment company. I have developed a cross-divisional initiative to adapt validated test items for program assessments. I have also written and taught assessment workshops. I developed an instructional matrix of test prep lessons for new program's Pupil Editions, grades 1–6; built a test-taking scope and sequence, developed test-taking strategies, created writers' guidelines, and wrote content. I am responsible for customization of Pupil and Teacher Edition pages for target states, grades 1–6. I developed and managed new instructional state-specific test prep components.

Before that, I worked for Reading Right in San Diego, CA. I worked there from 1997 to 2002 as an editor. I participated in the editorial process from inception to bound book. I also hired freelancers, created specifications, and edited copy. I created a seven-book series for CA and wrote open-ended questions, as well as scoring rubrics. I produced a seven-book Test Prep series in two months, generating $2 million in sales. I was promoted to senior editor and received recognition from the regional sales manager.

I earned my M.A. in Assessment from Miami University in Miami, OH. I earned my B.A. in Liberal Studies from Hudson University in New York, NY.

## Document #2:

### ARGIE RUIZ

17 West Main Street, Apt. 4B, Salt Lake City, UT 84101    801-555-5555
argieruiz@gmail.com

### CAREER SUMMARY

Accomplished editorial manager with more than ten years
of experience in editing, writing, and education.
Developer of instructional, basal, and supplementary materials,
formative assessments, and state-specific alignments in reading,
social studies, mathematics, and science, K–12.

### PROFESSIONAL EXPERIENCE

**The Leading Learning Edge    Salt Lake City, UT**

2002–present

#### Senior Editor

**Assessment Group:** *Manager of a new group developing state-specific materials for all content areas, as well as all national* *assessment components and state customizations for new reading program. Duties include product development; work with marketing, ad hoc groups, and focus test groups; hire and train staff, oversee editorial process; produce market-driven products.*

- Responsible for research, product development, and management of all national and state-specific reading assessments, K–6, in compliance with NCLB, including screening, diagnostic, progress monitoring tools, formative and summative assessments, fluency, and running record materials.
- Initiated a successful corporate partnership with an early reading assessment company.
- Developed a cross-divisional initiative to adapt validated test items for program assessments.
- Wrote and taught assessment workshops.
- Developed an instructional matrix of test prep lessons for new program's Pupil Editions, grades 1–6; built a test-taking scope and sequence, test-taking strategies, writers' guidelines, wrote content.
- Responsible for customization of Pupil and Teacher Edition pages for target states, grades 1–6.
- Developed and managed new, instructional state-specific test prep components.

**Reading Right    San Diego, CA**                    1997–2002

**Editor**

*Participated in the editorial process from inception to bound book. Hired freelancers, created specifications, edited copy.*

- Created seven-book series for CA and wrote open-ended questions, as well as scoring rubrics.
- Produced a seven-book Test Prep series in two months, generating $2 million in sales. Promoted to senior editor and received recognition from regional sales manager.

## EDUCATION

**M.A., Assessment,** Miami University, Miami, OH
**B.A. Liberal Studies,** Hudson University, New York, NY

Both documents have the same information, give or take a word or two. The information is ordered in the same way, too, in reverse chronological order. Nonetheless, the second document is much easier to read. *Much easier*. Why? The readability is affected by the document design.

## Introduction to Document Design

*Document design* refers to the way information is arranged and displayed. With even the most basic computer software programs, you have a dazzling array of options when it comes to document design, including font size and style, boldface, italics, bullets, numbers, color, clip art, margins—and much more. Your choices in these areas and your placement of each element can encourage or discourage people from processing your message. You want your writing to be read and understood. Therefore, you are going to want to make your document inviting and easy to read.

You are also going to make your documents conform to the expectations of the specific type of professional writing you are doing. For instance, a résumé such as the second example shown earlier in this chapter must be presented in a set format, with specific headings, subheadings, and indentations.

In this chapter, I am assuming that you have free reign to choose the elements of document design you will use. If you are working within a corporation, however, your choices may be constrained by the company style. In that case, you will format your documents into the templates the company provides for that purpose.

Follow these guidelines as you get started designing professional-looking documents:

### Plan the Design from the Very Beginning
After you analyze your purpose and audience, the next step is deciding on a design. Before you even start writing, carefully consider how you will organize and display the information. Ask yourself questions like these:

- How will people use the information?

- Will they read it from start to finish or just skim it? Thus, do I need to include a table of contents?

- Will they look for specific parts only?

- Will they refer to the document over and over (as in a manual) or read it just once?

- How much do they know about the topic? Do I have to provide ample headings and subheadings to guide them through the information, for instance?

- Will they read the document in hard copy (on paper) or on a computer screen?

### Choose a Design That Fits Your Document
In general, your document design should meet your reader's expectations. Readers have set expectations for standard documents such as letters, résumés, and memos, for example. If you don't know how to format a specific document such as a résumé, letter, or memo, start with one of the templates provided in software programs. These templates are basic outlines that show you how to arrange your material step-by-step. They provide an excellent springboard for designing professional documents.

## Keep It Simple

When in doubt, less is more. Just because you have so many choices of fonts and colors, for instance, doesn't mean that you have to use them all. In addition, you'll impress your readers and win their gratitude if you provide just the information they need in a format they find easy to read because it is familiar.

## Place the Main Points First

Unless you are presenting bad news in a letter or memo, present your key points in the first paragraph. This makes it more likely that your audience will read your message. It also shows your consideration of their time.

## Keep the Design Consistent

A set pattern makes a document easier to read; a changing pattern confuses readers. Consistency helps readers know when a section is beginning and when one is ending, for instance.

## Make the design obvious

Readers process information most easily when they understand how it is arranged. We make sense of what we are reading by relating parts to one another. Help your readers understand your text by using such obvious design elements as numbers, headings, lists, bullets, and a table of contents.

One great way to make a design obvious and easy to follow is to use the same design elements for related elements. For example, make all major heads boldface and capital letters in a 14-point type. Make all subheadings boldface, a mix of capital letters and lowercase letters in 12-point type. Place parallel elements in the same position on the page, too. For instance, all major heads might be centered; all subheads might be flush left. Here is a brief example. Notice how the design makes the document easier to read.

## Faculty Annual Report
June 1, 2006–May 30, 2007

**Name**        *Laurie Rozakis, Ph.D.*

### I. TEACHING
### Academic Advising and Counseling
I help many students who are preparing job search materials. I advise and counsel former as well as current students how to target companies, research the firms they are interested in, write targeted cover letters, prepare scannable résumés, and follow up with thank-you notes after interviews.

### B. Innovative Teaching and/or Experimental Teaching
Increasingly, my emphasis has been on integrating technology into my course work. I have accomplished this by setting up and maintaining my own Web site at htpp://members.aol.com/Rozakile/.

### C. Workshops and Seminars on Teaching
* *North Middle School, Martinsburg, West Virginia*       4/26/07
* *Nassau Library System Workshop: Three Facets of Technology*       9/12/06
* *Writing Across the Curriculum*       5/12/06

### D. Laboratory Development Activities
I continue to maximize my students' use of the Writing Center, a writing laboratory that offers students of all abilities an opportunity to receive intensive, individualized help with various types of writing.

### E. Awards for Teaching Performance
I received the Chancellor's Award for Teaching Excellence in 1994.

### G. Teaching Effectiveness (peer and student evaluation)
I use an evaluation form I developed after our last self-study, based on suggestions from the external reviewers. My student evaluations are universally excellent.

## II. SCHOLARSHIP

### A. Books
* *Be a Super Test Taker*                                February 2007
* *McGraw-Hill's Guide to Praxis, 2<sup>nd</sup> edition*        Spring 2007
* *Shaums' Guide to Research Papers, 2<sup>nd</sup> edition*    Spring 2007
* *The Portable Jewish Mother*                           March 2007
* *Macmillan McGraw-Hill's Social Studies*                 Fall 2006

### B. Videos
Video-Aided Instruction                                      2007

### C. Presentations
* *1st Farmingdale Conference on Technology*              4/26/07
* *Guest speaker at Farmingdale Rotary*                  11/28/06
* *Harborfields High School National Honor Society
  Induction Ceremony 2006*                              10/26/06

### D. Grants
*NY UUP Campus Grant*                                   June 2006

### E. Professional Workshops, Seminars, Public Lectures
* *Interview with Jim Bresnahan, WREL-AM News/Talk,
  Lexington, VA*                                          5/24/07
* *Interview with Chris Greenert, KSPI Morning Show,
  Stillwater, OK*                                         5/22/07
* "She Knows from Nice" by Judith H. Bernstein,
  *Newsday*                                               5/9/007
* *Jessie & Shotgun Show, CBS Radio KELI-FM,
  Denver, CO*                                             4/19/07
* "Maybe I Shud Go Bak Too Skul," Todd Venezia, reporter,
  *New York Post*                                         12/8/06

Now let's examine some specific design choices in greater detail. Think of this section as your menu of choices!

## Headings

Headings are a powerful design tool in a professional document because they establish the main ideas. As a result, headings direct your readers to the key points they must consider. Follow these guidelines with headings:

### Design Headings to Indicate Rank

Use style, color, and placement to make the ranking clear. To clarify the ranking as you design each document, think of your headings as an outline, like this:

    I. Main idea
        A. Subheading
        B. Subheading
            1. Example
            2. Example

    II. Main idea
        A. Subheading
        B. Subheading
            1. Example
            2. Example

    III. Main idea
        A. Subheading
        B. Subheading
            1. Example
            2. Example

Here's how this ranking might look transformed into a document design. Note the use of font size (14 for the main headings, 12 for the subheadings and examples), boldface (for the main ideas and subheadings), and italics (for the examples). Also note how the main ideas and subheadings are flush left (they are placed on the left margin) but the examples are indented 5 spaces. You can distinguish among the major and minor points in the text at a glance.

**Main idea**
**Subheading**
**Subheading**
   *Example*
   *Example*

**Main idea**
**Subheading**
**Subheading**
   *Example*
   *Example*

**Main idea**
**Subheading**
**Subheading**
   *Example*
   *Example*

### *Make the Headings Clear and Precise*
Don't make readers guess about the contents of each section. Instead, tell them directly.

### *Make the Headings Parallel*
Parallel structure means matching ideas of the same rank in the same (parallel) grammatical structure: parallel words, phrases, clauses, and sentences. Parts of speech must be parallel: nouns to nouns, verbs to verbs, and so on. Here are some examples:

| Not parallel: | TV news, movies, and watching sports |
| Parallel Nouns: | TV <u>news,</u> <u>movies,</u> and <u>sports listings</u> |
| Not parallel: | Installing the equipment and to configure the software |
| Parallel clauses: | <u>Installing the equipment</u> and <u>configuring the software</u> |

Parallel structures make your headings—and all your professional writing—sound smooth. Faulty parallelism sounds awkward and jarring. There's more on parallel structure in chapter 4.

### Following Headings with Text

Avoid placing headings one after the other without some intervening text. This is just plain logic: why have a heading without any text following it?

In typography, a *dingbat* is a symbol or ornament. You may also have heard them called "wingdings." Here are some attractive ones: ⌘ ❖ ☜ ☞ ✳ & ℘

## Highlighting

Here I'm defining highlighting as anything that sets off a text, including:

- ALTERNATE FONTS
- **boldface**
- CAPITALIZATION
- highlighting with a color or a shading.
- *italics*
- "quotation marks"
- <u>underscoring</u>

Follow these guidelines as you decide what to highlight:

### Highlight Only Really Important Words

When too much is highlighted, nothing is highlighted. Your reader stops paying attention because too much is called out.

### Keep It Simple and Consistent

As you read earlier in this chapter, stick with what readers have come to expect. You can use whatever highlighting you feel best suits your design, of course. Here are some conventions to get you started working within readers' expectations:

Alternate fonts
- If you do decide to use alternate fonts, keep it simple. Use a standard font such as Courier. Avoid fancy fonts such as *this one*, *this one*, and **THIS ONE** in professional text.

Boldface
- Use boldface for commands, such as "Do **not** remove the flash drive before checking the Off button" or "Type **visitor** and press the **enter** key."
- Use boldface for the headings of tables and charts.
- Use boldface for the initial word in a label or special notice, such as **Danger!**

Capitalization
- Most people find headings written in all capital letters distracting and difficult to read. They tend to associate it with "flaming" (using insulting or overly strong language in e-mail), so I advise avoiding their use.

Highlighting with a color or shading
- Color is easy to use on screen, and you see it all the time. Hypertext links, for instance, are usually highlighted on the screen in blue.
- However, color is difficult to use with printed documents because of its cost. Keep this in mind if you decide that you want to use color.
- If you want to use color, plan it carefully. For instance, readers won't automatically remember your choice of color schemes, such as green for major heads, red for subheads, and so on.
- Color is one of the most frequently abused highlighting features because it's so much fun to use. After all, who wouldn't want a brightly-colored

online document? It's so pretty! But remember:
Pretty doesn't translate to easy to read—or easy to
print. You want easy to read.

## Italics
- Use italics for simple emphasis, as in "Do *not* turn
  the key unless the vehicle is in Park."
- Use italics to set off definitions.
- Use italics for figure titles and labels, as in *fig 1-3.*

## Quotation Marks
- Use quotation marks to set off definitions.
- Use quotation marks for quoted speech, numbers,
  letters, or words referred to as such—in short, the
  traditional, accepted use of quotation marks.
- Avoid single quotation marks. They are considered
  a pretentious affectation and should not be used.

## Underscoring
- Underscoring (also called underlining) is rarely
  used today, although this technique was very
  popular in the day of typewriters.
- Underlining tends to look old-fashioned and frumpy
  in today's well-designed professional writing.

## Mixed Use
- You can use a combination of boldface, color, and a
  different font for headings.
- However, I rarely advise writers to mix too many
  techniques because it invariably makes the document difficult to read.

While you're mulling over your wealth of design choices, take
a look at a variety of different professional writing. See which
designs you like, and which ones you don't. Then adapt those
design techniques to your own documents.

And don't forget to set up a style sheet for each document

you design so you can remember what design choices you made.

## Lists

As you can tell from this book, I like lists! That's because they make it easier for readers to read a text quickly and get the main points. You can set off your lists with numbers, bullets, dingbats, or other design features. Which ones should you use? Use numbered lists in directions or instructions, when the items must be presented in chronological order from first to last.

Do . . .
- Keep each entry short, no more than a sentence.
- Keep all items parallel.
- Omit words such as "a," "an," and "the" at the beginning of each entry.
- Experiment with column format. Some lists work better in one column; others, in two columns.

Don't . . .
- Mix numbers and bullets in the same list. You get one or the other.
- Include more than 5 to 10 items in the list. If you include any more entries, your readers are apt to get lost.

## Visuals

Visuals come in many varieties, including:

| | | | |
|---|---|---|---|
| diagrams | drawings | photographs | charts |
| graphs | tables | clip art | maps |

As with headings, choose the visuals that most clearly help you communicate your message. Following are some guidelines to consider as you plan what visuals—if any—to include in your professional documents.

Drawings are especially helpful with instructions because they illustrate the process. Photographs are often used in reports to show people, places, and things. No matter what visuals you use, ensure the following:

- Make the visual large enough so that it can be seen. This is especially important with visuals that have fine detail, such as maps.
- Suit the visual to your audience and purpose. On one hand, your visual shouldn't be too complex for a lay audience. On the other hand, it can't be too elementary for a technically savvy reader.
- Integrate the visual in the text. Don't just plop it in; make sure that it really matters to the text and that you have discussed it in the text.
- Label each visual so your reader understands what purpose it serves. The label should be placed right next to the visual.
- Include titles to clarify tables and other charts.
- Place the visual at point of use. Readers get annoyed and frustrated when they have to flip through documents to match visuals with text.
- Give credit for any graphic that you have taken from a source, including tables, photographs, illustrations, charts, graphs, and so on. Be extra careful not to violate copyright laws. Some visuals can be used freely; other cannot.

## Templates

So many choices! So little time! What's a beginning writer of professional documents to do? It's easy: use templates. I mentioned templates earlier in this book and this chapter.

Templates are nothing more than patterns. They have all the formatting, fonts, spacing, and so on built right in. All you have to do is keyboard over the instructions and voilà! You have a beautifully formatted professional document. Until you practice a lot of design choices on your own, using templates is a quick, easy, and effective way to create attractive documents that will help your readers process your message.

Templates are included in software packages. Just use the keyword "templates" to find them in your software program. You'll find templates for a variety of documents, including résumés, reports, memos, letters, and Web pages.

# CHAPTER 4

## Achieve a Professional Style

**YOU MUST REMEMBER THIS**
Style refers to an author's distinctive way of writing. Style includes the words, phrases, sentences, document design, and tone you use in your writing.

**ALL THE RIGHT MOVES**
As a skilled professional writer, you will adjust your style to suit your audience and purpose.

In previous chapters, you learned how you make choices every time you sit down to write. One of the most important choices you make is your writing style. Professional writing has a very distinctive style, as you will learn in this chapter.

### Writers Use Different Styles

Compare these two different texts. See how they are the same and different from each other:

THE RAINBOW

My heart leaps up when I behold
  A rainbow in the sky:
So was it when my life began;

> So is it now I am a man;
> So be it when I shall grow old,
>   Or let me die!
> The child is father of the man;
> And I could wish my days to be
> Bound each to each by natural piety.
>
>               —William Wordsworth

Sunlight is made of varying wavelengths of light. Light with short wavelengths looks blue, violet, and indigo. Light with long wavelengths looks red, orange, and yellow. When sunlight enters a raindrop, the light reflects off the back of the raindrop and emerges in the same direction. The emerging light creates a rainbow.

These texts are the same in that they share the same topic: rainbows. Nonetheless, each passage is vastly different because of its style. The poem has many figures of speech and non-literal language. You must "read between the lines" and make inferences to understand the writer's message. The second passage has short sentences and simple words. The message is straightforward.

Which style is best? It all depends on your purpose and audience. Thus, I can't teach you a "one size fits all" style when it comes to writing professional documents. However, I *can* give you some guidelines that will work in many of the most common professional writing situations.

Since much of professional writing is done in groups, it is important that you and your colleagues achieve a seamless style, so the reader cannot tell where one writer ended and the next one started. Indeed, the audience should not even realize that perhaps more than one writer had a hand in the creation of the document.

## Overview of a Professional Writing Style

You learned that you have many choices to make when you write professional documents. The following chart shows some of these choices:

| Stylistic Element | Professional Writing Style |
|---|---|
| Words | Choose words that suit the audience's level of knowledge and expertise. Use professional words and terms (*jargon*) when they are expected by your audience. |
| Sentences | In most instances, keep your sentences brief, no more than 15 words long. |
| Paragraphs | Generally, keep your paragraphs brief, usually around 3 to 5 sentences each. |
| Ideas | Generally, place your key ideas in the very beginning of your document—including all recommendations and conclusions. |
| Voice | Use the active voice to be clear and concise. Use the passive voice when you want to avoid assigning blame. |
| Transitions | Use a lot of transitions—linking words and phrases—to help your audience follow your ideas. Number the steps in instructions and directions. |
| Parallelism | Make all sentence elements parallel whenever possible. |
| Tone | Use the appropriate tone when writing for people above you (supervisors, etc.), on your level (friends, neighbors, colleagues), and below you (employees, children). |
| Wordiness | Be concise. Omit any unnecessary words and phrases. |
| Document Design | Include visuals and other design elements to make your writing easy to read and understand. |

Some of these elements we've discussed in previous chapters, so let's explore the rest of these important choices now.

## Be Clear

The first rule of good professional writing is clarity. After all, your document will be useless if your audience can't understand it. Here are some ways to achieve clarity.

*Use the Appropriate Sentence Form*
There are four types of sentences in English: *declarative, exclamatory, interrogative,* and *imperative.*

- *Declarative sentences* state an idea. They end with a period. Use declarative sentences in professional writing to explain, show, or tell. Declarative sentences will be the most common form you use in professional writing.
  **Example:** There are two basic types of stethoscopes.

- *Interrogative sentences* ask a question. They end with a question mark. Use interrogative sentences to ask questions, which will be rare in professional writing.
  **Example:** Do you know how to measure blood pressure?

- *Exclamatory sentences* show strong emotions. They end with an exclamation mark. Use exclamatory sentences in professional writing with warnings, cautions, and other important safety elements.
  **Examples:** Put that instrument down carefully!
  Warning!
  Caution!

- *Imperative sentences* give orders or directions. They end with a period or an exclamation mark. Use imperative sentences in professional writing when you write directions and instructions.
  **Example:** Inflate the cuff to about 40 mm Hg above the level at which the radial pulse disappears.

*Use the Appropriate Sentence Structure*

Sentences in English can also be classified according to the type of clauses and the number of clauses they contain. *Clauses* are groups of words that have a subject and a verb. *Independent clauses* are complete sentences. *Dependent clauses* are fragments. They cannot stand alone; they can only be part of a sentence.

- *Simple sentences* have one independent clause.
  **Example:** <u>The maximum allowable concentration is ten parts H2S per million parts breathable air.</u>
  Independent clause

- *Compound sentences* have two or more independent clauses joined by the conjunctions *for, and, nor, but, or, yet, so.*
  **Example:** <u>The meeting is tomorrow</u> and
  Independent clause
  <u>everyone is expected to attend.</u>
  Independent clause

- *Complex sentences* have one independent clause and one dependent clause.
  **Example:** <u>Although a majority of coffee drinkers consider it a stimulant,</u>
  Dependent clause
  <u>many people say that caffeine actually has a paradoxical effect.</u>
  Independent clause

- *Compound-complex sentences* have two or more independent clauses and one dependent clause.
  **Example:** <u>Since the early artificial heart pumps were cumbersome</u>
  Dependent clause

  <u>and they tended to obstruct the flow of blood to the right atrium,</u> Independent clause

  <u>scientists created more effective alternatives.</u>
  Independent clause

In general, use simple sentences to write most clearly and directly to general audiences. You can use longer and more complex structures with more sophisticated, technical audiences, but even here, the more complex the topic, the shorter and easier your sentences should be. This creates a considerate style, making it easier for your readers to follow the ideas.

No doubt, this is the opposite style of what you were taught in high school and college. There, you were likely encouraged to use long, complex, and compound-complex sentences to create a richer, more allusive style. In professional writing, however, simpler sentences are far preferred in nearly all cases.

## Use the Active and Passive Voice Correctly

- In the active voice, the subject performs the action.
  **Example:** Sanjay will present his research at the conference.

- In the passive voice, the subject receives the action expressed in the verb; the subject is acted upon. The agent performing the action may appear in a "by . . ." phrase or may be omitted.
  **Examples:** The research will be presented at the conference by Sanjay.
  The research will be presented at the conference.

As you can see from these examples, the active voice is stronger, more direct, and less wordy than the passive voice. This creates a more considerate, readable style. As a result, it is usually far preferable to use the active voice.

But . . . use the passive voice when you want to avoid placing blame:

Active:  You made a mistake.
Passive: A mistake was made.

Active:  The administrative staff attempted to solve the problem but was unsuccessful.
Passive: Attempts were made to solve the problem but were unsuccessful.

> In general, use the active voice to achieve a concise and vigorous style. Use the passive voice to avoid assigning blame. This helps people avoid embarrassment and "save face."

### Use Parallel Structure

*Parallelism* means matching grammatical structures: nouns to nouns, verbs to verbs, phrases to phrases, clauses to clauses, and so on. Parallelism is a powerful stylistic tool in professional writing because it helps you put ideas of the same importance in the same format. This makes your writing clear and smooth. Here's a bonus: parallelism also makes your message memorable. Consider the following literary example:

> It was the best of times, it was the worst of times, it was the age of wisdom, it was the age of foolishness, it was the epoch of belief, it was the epoch of incredulity, it was the season of Light, it was the season of Darkness, it was the spring of hope, it was the winter of despair, we had everything before us, we had nothing before us, we were all going direct to Heaven, we were all going direct the other way—in short, the

period was so far like the present period, that some of its noisiest authorities insisted on its being received, for good or for evil, in the superlative degree of comparison only.

Now consider the following professional memo. Notice how the parallelism makes the memo clear and easy to read.

Below is the department meeting schedule for fall 2007. All meetings are held on Tuesdays at 11:00 in Knapp 33:

      Tuesday, September 11
      Tuesday, October 16
      Tuesday, November 13
      Tuesday, December 4

Please make note of these dates.

Thank you.

## Be Correct

Professional writing represents not only you but also the company or organization for which you work. As a result, it must be letter-perfect. The following section describes some common grammatical problems and shows you how to correct them.

### Make Sure Pronoun and Antecedents Agree

A pronoun replaces a noun. To make sure that your writing is clear, always use the noun first before using the pronoun. Also be sure that the pronoun refers directly to the noun. Pronouns and antecedents (the words to which they refer) must agree or match. Follow these rules:

- Use a singular personal pronoun with a singular indefinite pronoun.
  **Example:** If *anyone* has questions, refer *him* or *her* to Human Resources.
  (The singular pronouns *him* and *her* refer to the singular pronoun *anyone.*)

- Use a plural personal pronoun with a plural indefinite pronoun.
  **Example:** If *they* have questions, refer *them* to Human Resources.
  (The plural pronoun *they* refers to the plural pronoun *them.*)

*Use the Correct Case*

Case is the form of a noun or pronoun that shows how it is used in a sentence. English has three cases: *nominative, objective,* and *possessive.*

- Use the nominative case to show the subject of a verb.
  **Example:** *We* spoke to the agent about the deal.

- Use the objective case to show the noun or pronoun receives the action.
  **Example:** The agent was willing to speak to *us.*

- Use the possessive case to show ownership.
  **Example:** The agent gave *us* his advice.

The following chart shows the three cases:

| Nominative | Objective | Possessive |
|---|---|---|
| (Pronoun as subject) | (Pronoun as objective) | (Ownership) |
| I | me | my, mine |
| you | you | your, yours |
| he | him | his |
| she | her | her, hers |
| it | it | its |
| we | us | our, ours |
| they | them | their, theirs |
| who | whom | whose |
| whoever | whomever | whoever |

*Don't Confuse Contractions with Possessive Pronouns*

Contractions are two words combined. When you contract words, add an apostrophe in the space where the letters have been taken out.

| **Examples:** | does + not = | doesn't |
|---|---|---|
| | we + are = | we're |
| | I + will = | I'll |

Study this chart:

| Contraction | Possessive Pronoun |
|---|---|
| it's (it is) | its |
| you're (you are ) | your |
| they're (they are) | their |
| who's (who is) | whose |

*Avoid Sexist Language*

Sexist language assigns qualities to people on the basis of their gender. This language discriminates against people by limiting what they can do. Here are some guidelines:

- Avoid using *he* to refer to both men and women.

- Avoid using *man* to refer to both men and women.

- Avoid language that denigrates people, such as lady lawyer (use *lawyer*), male nurse (use *nurse*), waitress (use *server*), stewardess (use *flight attendant*).

*Use Possessive Forms Correctly*
Possession means "ownership." Follow these rules to create possessive nouns:

- With singular nouns, add an apostrophe and an *s*.
  **Examples:**    report       report's cover page
  company    company's policies

- With plural nouns ending in *s*, add an apostrophe after the s.
  **Examples:**    reports      reports' cover page
  companies    companies' policies

- With plural nouns not ending in *s*, add an apostrophe and an s.
  **Examples:**    women      women's room
  mice    mice's tails

- To show possession for possessive pronouns, don't use an apostrophe
  **Examples:** This seat is <u>yours.</u>
  Possessive pronoun

The computer is <u>theirs,</u> not <u>ours.</u>
Possessive    Possessive
pronoun     pronoun

Some people add an 's with plural nouns ending in s, as in *reports's pages*. I favor leaving off the second s. Follow your company's style, but if you work on your own or your company doesn't have a set grammar and usage style sheet, be consistent. Either always add the s or never do.

## Don't Confuse Words!

English has many words that are often confused. Here are fifty of the most common ones. Use this list to help you make sure that you've used the precise words you need in each and every document.

1. *accept:* to take
   *except:* to leave out; to exclude

2. *advise:* to guide (verb)
   *advice:* guidance (noun)

3. *air:* atmosphere (noun)
   *err:* to make a mistake (verb)

4. *affect:* to influence (verb)
   *affect:* a psychological state (noun)
   *effect:* impact and purpose (noun)

5. *a lot:* many
   *allot:* divide

6. *altar:* platform upon which religious rites are performed
   *alter:* to change

7. *allowed:* given permission
   *aloud:* out loud, verbally

8. *all together:* all at one time
   *altogether:* completely

9. *already:* previously
   *all ready:* completely prepared

10. *allusion:* reference to a famous person, place, event, work of art, or work of literature
    *illusion:* misleading appearance; deception

11. *among:* three or more people, places, or things
    *between:* two people, places, or things

12. *amount:* things that <u>can't</u> be counted
    *number:* things that <u>can</u> be counted

13. *are:* plural verb
    *our:* belonging to us

14. *ascent:* to move up
    *assent:* to agree

15. *bare:* undressed
    *bare:* unadorned; plain
    *bear:* animal
    *bear:* to carry; to hold

16. *base:* bottom part of an object; plate in baseball; morally low
    *bass:* lowest male voice; musical instrument
    *bass:* type of fish

17. *beau:* sweetheart
    *bow:* loops of ribbon; device used to propel arrows
    *bow:* to bend from the waist; forward end of a ship

18. *berth:* sleeping area in a ship
    *birth:* being born

19. *board:* thin piece of wood; group of directors
    *bored:* uninterested

20. *born:* native; brought forth by birth
    *borne:* endured (past participle of "to bear")

21. *bore:* tiresome person
    *boar:* male pig

22. *brake:* device for slowing a vehicle
    *break:* to crack or destroy

23. *bread:* baked goods
    *bred:* reared or born

24. *breadth:* side-to-side dimension
    *breath:* inhalation and exhalation

25. *buy:* to purchase
    *by:* near; next to

26. *capital:* official seat of government; highly important; net
        worth of a business
    *capitol:* state government buildings
    *Capitol:* building in Washington, D.C., where U.S. Congress
        meets

27. *conscience:* moral sense
    *conscious:* awake

28. *cent:* penny
    *scent:* aroma

29. *cheep:* what a bird says
    *cheap:* inexpensive

30. *deer:* animal
    *dear:* beloved

31. *draft:* breeze
    *draft:* sketch

32. *dye:* change color
    *die:* to cease living

33. *emigrate:* to move away from one's country
    *immigrate:* to move to another country

34. *eminent:* distinguished
    *imminent:* expected momentarily
    *immanent:* inborn; inherent

35. *fare:* price charged for transporting a passenger
    *fair:* not biased; moderately large; moderately good

36. *gorilla:* ape
    *guerrilla:* soldier

37. *grate:* to irritate; to reduce to small pieces
    *great:* big; wonderful

38. *hair:* stuff on your head
    *heir:* beneficiary

39. *here:* in this place
    *hear:* to listen

40. *hour:* sixty-minute period
    *our:* belonging to us

41. *it's:* contraction for *it is*
    *its:* possessive pronoun

42. *lay:* to put down
    *lie:* to be flat; untruth; to tell an untruth

43. *lead:* to conduct
    *lead:* bluish-gray metal
    *led:* past tense of *to lead*

44. *loose:* not tight; not fastened (noun)
    *loose:* to untighten; to let go (verb)
    *lose:* to misplace (verb)

45. *peace:* calm
    *piece:* section

46. *plain:* not beautiful; obvious
    *plane:* airplane

47. *presence:* company; closeness
    *presents:* gifts

48. *principal:* main; head of a school
    *principle:* rule

49. *than:* comparison
    *then:* at that time

50. *their:* belonging to them
    *they're:* contraction for *they are*
    *there:* place

## Be Concise

With professional writing, it's especially critical that you write simply and directly. That's because you don't want to waste your reader's time. Neither do you want to confuse your reader with unnecessary words and phrases. As a result, omit unnecessary details or ideas that you have already stated. Use a lot of important detail, but no unnecessary words.

William Strunk, Jr., a famous stylist, gave this advice: "Vigorous writing is concise. A sentence should contain no unnecessary words, a paragraph no unnecessary sentences, for the same reason that a drawing should have no unnecessary lines and a machine no unnecessary parts. This requires that the writer make all his sentences short, or that he avoid all detail and treat his subjects only in outline, but that every word tell."

# CHAPTER 5

## Learn the Writing Process

—————•◦•—————

**YOU MUST REMEMBER THIS**

Many writers find it helpful to follow a specific series of steps when they compose professional documents. Using this process can make your writing easier and better.

**ALL THE RIGHT MOVES**

Every time you compose a professional document, first determine your purpose (reason for writing) and audience (readers). Second, gather information. Third, organize the information. Fourth, write the first draft. Fifth, revise and edit the draft.

B y now, your head is probably spinning with all the new information that I've given you! So far, you've learned how professional writing differs from writing you do for school or personal communication. You've explored what qualities differentiate professional writing from everyday writing and school writing. You've read about the importance of audience and purpose to all professional documents. You've explored design elements and stylistic considerations as well. Before I show you how to write specific types of professional documents—instructions, letters, résumés, e-mails, reports, and so on—let's take a look at how professional writers actually write.

## Personal Writing Inventory

First, what steps do you follow when *you* write? Assume that you had to do one of the following tasks:

- Write a memo to your boss about a late shipment
- Revise your résumé so you can apply for a new job
- Compose a report for your colleagues on the PTA about buying new playground equipment
- Write the minutes for this month's Homeowners' Association meeting
- Write a letter of recommendation to a college for a teenager who has been a scout in your troop for five years
- Answer some e-mails from customers

Most writers follow the steps in this order:

1. Determine purpose and audience
2. Gather information
3. Organize information
4. Write first draft
5. Revise and edit draft

However, the process is not linear. In fact, most people go back and forth among the steps as they write. For example, you will likely revise and edit as you write your first draft, as well as all subsequent drafts. That's why this is often called a *recursive process.*

Most people find that following the steps in the writing process helps them:

- Relieve anxiety about writing
- Get started writing and avoid "writer's block"
- Write more quickly and easily
- Produce better professional documents

Thinking about how you write—the process of *metacognition*—can help you analyze which writing techniques work best for you . . . and which ones don't. Use the information in this chapter to help you scrutinize the way that you write.

Some people add a sixth step: publishing. This can refer to sharing your document with anyone in any form—as a letter, blog, Web page, e-mail, report, speech, and so on.

## Step #1: Determine Your Purpose and Audience

A well-known writer once said, "Writers keep surprising themselves . . . they don't know what they are saying until they see it on the page." This may very well be true when it comes to writing novels, short stories, poems, journals, personal letters, and blogs, but not when it comes to professional writing. When you're composing professional documents, there shouldn't be any surprises. That's because you're not writing for your own pleasure or to entertain someone. Rather, professional writing is designed to explain or persuade a specific group of readers, as you learned earlier in this book.

The process of producing a professional document is often called "content creation" rather than "writing." The term *content creation* reflects the importance of focusing on your purpose and audience and satisfying their needs in professional writing. Remember:

- Your *purpose* is why you are writing (to persuade or to explain).

- Your *audience* is the people who will read your writing, such as your supervisor, coworkers, shareholders, community members, and so on.

## Revisiting Purpose

Your *purpose* may be something as straightforward as helping your readers understand the details of a technical process, or perhaps taking a particular action using that system. For instance, if some bank employees are not posting deposits to accounts in the correct manner, you might be asked to write a document instructing them how to perform the procedure correctly. Similarly, the manager of a small store in a mall might wonder which of two locations within the mall would be a better choice for a satellite kiosk, so you might be asked to study the market and write a report with recommendations. Or, you might be a product designer who needs to write the FAQs to explain how to navigate the company's new Web site. You might be the president of the community association and need to write a white paper explaining why your group has been formed and what it intends to accomplish.

In each of these instances, the writer—you!—is conveying knowledge to satisfy a specific need (purpose) for specific people who need it (audience). This is your first task every time you sit down to write a professional document.

A white paper is an essay that states an organization's position or philosophy about a social issue, political situation, or other subject. A white paper can also be an explanation of an architecture, framework, or product technology. Typically, a white paper explains the results, conclusions, or construction resulting from some organized committee or research collaboration or design and development effort.

We've discussed purpose in chapter 2, but now I'd like you to look at it in more depth. Therefore, ask yourself the following questions to pinpoint your purpose:

- Do you want to *analyze* (break a process into its parts)?

- Do you want to *define* (explain the origin of a word, for instance)?

- Do you want to *describe* (use the five senses to help readers visualize a person, place, thing, or idea)?

- Do you want to *evaluate* (judge something to show its strengths and weaknesses)?

- Do you want to *explain* (give details, examples, and illustrations)?

- Do you want to *classify* (sort and catalog)?

- Do you want to *compare* (show similarities)?

- Do you want to *contrast* (show differences)?

- Do you want to *compare and contrast* (show similarities and differences)?

- Do you want to give *instructions or directions* (process analysis or "how to" documents)?

- Do you want to *trace a process* in order from first to last (use chronological order, the order of time)?

### *Revisiting Audience*

Remember that your *audience* affects many aspects of your written documents, including the words and visuals you choose, the style you select, and the organization you create. On one hand, a nontechnical audience won't understand a document that's heavy with jargon. They're likely to skim it or even toss it aside in a fury because it frustrates them so much. On the other hand, a technical audience is likely to need a great amount of detail because it is critical for their work.

Further, busy audiences won't have time to read an entire document, so the content must be organized for ease of searching. As a result, you usually place the key ideas up front, in the first paragraph or even the first sentence.

It's rare that something is "all" or "nothing." As a result, we infrequently speak in absolutes, preferring shades of meaning. However, when it comes to purpose and audience in relation to professional writing, I feel comfortable talking in absolutes. That's because regardless of the place, time, or specific task, *all* professional writing is *always* accomplished with a particular end in mind. As a result, you will *always* begin the process of writing a professional document by making sure that you have pinpointed your audience and know exactly what information they require.

## Step #2: Gather Information

When you sit down to write, does your mind abruptly go blank? Do you suddenly (and shockingly) discover that you don't have anything to say? Do you find something else to do, anything else to do, to avoid having to write? This happens to many people, especially when it comes to writing a professional document, because they know the pressure is on. You can relieve a lot of that pressure by gathering information. Getting the facts that you need helps you get right to work without feeling panic or resorting to procrastination.

Here are some effective ways to gather information:

*Set Up a Plan*
Make a plan every time you write any professional document longer than a one-paragraph e-mail. The plan helps you make sure that you'll have ample backup material if you can't locate the facts that you need in a timely fashion. This reduces panic, too.

Having a time line, for instance, helps you track all the information that you're seeking. Some people make a spreadsheet; others use a large whiteboard to track the arrival of important research documents. Your time line doesn't have to be as complex as a New York City transit map. Rather, it can be a simple calendar or flow chart. No matter what form you find most comfortable, creating a written plan for a professional document helps you avoid panic and gather facts.

## Research Information

Research can be classified as *primary* and *secondary*. Primary research is information that you collect through direct observation or experimentation. Secondary research, in contrast, is information that comes from someone else's research. Lab experiments you conduct are primary research; encyclopedia entries and newspaper articles are examples of secondary research. Use whatever kind of research will give you the information you need—information of absolute veracity. Here are some methods of researching information:

- Brainstorm ideas. Start with what you know; then you can figure out what you need to find.
- Ask yourself: Who? What? When? Where? Why? How? So What?
- Look at the topic from different angles.
- Interview reliable people, especially people who will read your document.
- Take surveys.
- Conduct experiments.
- Define any important terms. Use different reference sources to get different points of view.
- Read online journals, newspapers, magazines, and professional publications.
- Get pertinent statistics, facts, examples, and anecdotes.
- See if there are any relevant laws on the topic.
- Use books.

## Verify Information

One of the great strengths of a free press—both print and online—is its ability to print anything that does not libel its subject. However, that very freedom presents its own problems for you when you are finding information for your professional documents. *Just because a source appears in print, in the media, or online does not mean that it is valid.* As a result, you must carefully evaluate every source you find before you use it. This means that you must read critically and carefully.

Before you decide to use *any* source, you have to judge its reliability, credibility, and appropriateness. Use the following criteria as you determine whether a source is valid for inclusion in your document:

1. Authority

   Evaluate the information you find. After all, some sources *are* more reliable than others. That's because they were prepared with greater care by experts in the field and have been reviewed by scholars, teachers, and others we respect for their knowledge of the subject. As a result, they carry greater authority and will help you create valid and useful professional documents. Here are some guidelines to use:

   • Is the source complete, or have certain facts been cut for their controversial nature or for space limitations? Be suspicious of incomplete sources.

   • Does the author document his or her claims with other source materials? If the writer's claims can't be backed up, don't trust their assertions.

   • Is the author named? The author should be credited.

   • Does the person have a good reputation in this field? Look for an academic degree, an e-mail address at a college or university, a byline in a reputable newspaper, and/or a list of publications. Based on this information, can you conclude that the writer is qualified to write on this subject?

2. Source

As you evaluate the materials you locate, consider where the source comes from—its sponsoring agency, publisher, and so on. Here are some guidelines to use:

- Is the source reputable? Valid sources are well known; they appear on lists of recommended books or sites.

- Does the piece come from a place known for its authority, such as a reputable publisher or sponsored Web site? Steer clear of unknown or suspicious sources.

3. Timeliness

The material you use must be up-to-date. For example, you don't want statistics that are useless because they are outmoded. Timeliness is a crucial issue with Web sites, since cyberspace is cluttered with piles of outdated sites. Sometimes people post information and move on to something new. The site hangs out there, forgotten and woefully outdated. Always check the dates on any Web sites to find out when the material was posted and last updated.

4. Bias

Every source is biased, because every source has a point of view. Bias is not necessarily bad, as long as you recognize it as such and take it into account as you evaluate and use the source.

5. Purpose

Different sources are written for different reasons. For instance, scholarly or technical pieces usually aim to advance knowledge, while commercial Web sites are designed to sell products and services. Consider *why* the source was written as you evaluate it for possible inclusion in your professional document.

6. Appropriateness

The value of a source depends not only on its quality but also on its use to you in a specific writing situation. For a source to make the final cut, it has to fit with your audience, purpose, and tone. It must be *appropriate* to your document. Here are some guidelines to use:

- Do you understand the material in the source? If the source is too technical for you to grasp fully, you might not use it correctly in your document.

- Is the source written at a level appropriate to your audience?

- Does the source suit your purpose in the particular document you are writing?

- Does the source have the information you need?

Many sources you find won't be reliable or won't contain the information you need. Don't be discouraged; that's what gathering information is all about. Further, you'll want to verify facts (such as dates, statistics, and scientific experiments) by double-checking them. Be especially wary of online encyclopedias written by unnamed contributors, because the material can easily be corrupted by hackers. Further, the information tends to be unstable because it changes so often.

In summary, all sources are not equally valid. Be sure to evaluate every source you find carefully and completely before you decide whether to use it. Be especially wary of online sources; use only reputable articles. Weak or inaccurate sources can seriously damage your credibility as a writer.

## Step #3: Organize the Information

Create a visual that helps you decide where to place each piece of information to best achieve your purpose and appeal to your audience. There are many different types of visuals you can use, including outlines and story maps.

Here is an example of one possible way to organize a feasibility study:

I. Opening
 A. Brief introduction
 B. Conclusions
 C. Recommendations
II. Background information
III. Purpose
IV. Environmental impact
V. Rules and regulations
VI. Staffing: outsourcing and insourcing
VII. Projected cost
VIII. Anticipated profit
IX. Summary
X. Appendices, glossary

## Step #4: Write the First Draft

Now it's time to put your ideas into sentences and paragraphs. Here, focus on giving your audience the information they need. Some people say that you should ignore mechanics—such as spelling, punctuation, capitalization, and grammar—at this point. I strongly disagree because of the nature of professional writing.

### Anticipate the Best, but Plan for the Worst

With everyday writing, you usually have the luxury of letting your writing sit and "cool off." You can then return to it and

edit your ideas, revising your work and polishing it.
Unfortunately, with professional writing, you often don't have
as much time as you originally thought or were promised. The
time line has a mysterious way of getting shortened as the
town meeting gets moved up, the conference call with the
client occurs a day sooner, your boss insists on seeing your
document before you're really ready to share it. As a result, I
strongly suggest that you revise and edit as you draft.

Hope that you will have time to revise and edit thoroughly,
but always assume that you won't. Be ready to submit your document before the deadline.

*Give Credit to Sources*

You want to come across as the expert, the authoritative
source. Nonetheless, you must give credit to material that you
used from outside sources. Ironically, giving credit often makes
you look more credible because it shows that you took the
time to use only the highest quality sources. It shows that you
are familiar with the literature in your field; the history of the
problem, situation, or product; and the work of the other
experts.

> Plagiarism is using someone else's words without giving ade-
> quate credit.

## Step #5: Revise and Edit the Draft

*Revise* means "to look again." When you revise, you check for
problems in mechanics, of course: grammar, usage, spelling,
punctuation, and capitalization. You also check for problems
with logic, unity, and cohesion. You make sure that you have
completely satisfied your audience and achieved your purpose.
As a result, revising and editing involves:

- adding information
- deleting information
- moving information around
- correcting information

Revision is the key to effective professional documents. Here you think more deeply about your readers' needs and expectations. Ask yourself questions such as these:

- Is my writing concise? Have I eliminated any unnecessary words, phrases, and ideas?

- Is my writing correct? Have I corrected each and every error?

- Is my writing complete? For example, what do my readers need to know before they can understand something else? How much support will each idea need to convince my readers? Which terms should be defined for these particular readers?

- Is my organization effective? Are all my ideas linked in a logical fashion?

### Save Drafts

Don't overwrite when you revise and edit. Instead, save each successive draft as a new file, as in:

PTAminutes1.doc
PTAminutes2.doc
PTAminutes3.doc
PTAminutes4.doc

This way, if you want to refer to a previous draft, you'll have a copy of it. You'll often find that something you might have deleted can be repurposed in another part of this document, or even a new document.

## Run a Spell-check

Spell-checks are great because they can pick up a lot of typos. However, don't rely on them as the last word because they're just not that good yet. There's no substitute for a close proof-reading. If at all possible, let your document sit a day or even more before you proofread it again. This "cooling off" period allows you to look at your work with fresh eyes.

## Consider Peer-reviewing

Peer-reviewing (also called peer-editing) is the process where-by people work together to read, comment on, and recommend improvements on one another's work. It's natural to feel uncomfortable about criticizing someone else's work. For example, how do you tell a colleague that his or her document has a major flaw in logic? Here are some guidelines for effective peer-reviewing without undue pain:

- *Set the ground rules at the first meeting.*
  Tell your colleagues what aspects of the writing you think need attention, such as topic, audience, or purpose. In return, have colleagues whose work you are peer-reviewing supply you with information on their objectives and concerns.

- *Look at the entire document.*
  When you peer-review other people's writing, remember above all that you should consider all aspects of that writing, not just the mechanics (grammar, spelling, and punctuation). Read the draft several times, looking for a complete range of issues.

- *Be polite and collegial.*
  Try to avoid making comments or criticisms that are based on your own personal style. Base your criticisms and suggestions for improvements on generally accepted guidelines, concepts, and rules. If you do

make a comment that is really your own preference, explain it.

- *Be helpful.*
  Whenever you criticize something in the writer's draft, try to suggest some way to correct the problem. It's not enough to tell the writer that his or her paper seems disorganized, for example. Explain how that problem could be solved.

- *Be positive.*
  Be sure to include ample praise as well as constructive criticism. Find positive, encouraging things to say about the draft you're reviewing. Compliments, even small ones, are usually wildly appreciated. Read through the draft at least once looking for things that were done well, and then let the writer know about them.

You can also ask someone to edit, revise, and proofread for you. Naturally, be careful with political considerations here; you never want to appear unable to handle your own writing assignments, especially in a professional setting.

### Use Checklists

One of the most effective ways to revise and edit is to use a checklist. Make a new checklist for every document in order to zero in on exactly what elements matter most in that writing situation. Here are some sample checklists:

Sample Revising and Editing Checklist #1

| | |
|---|---|
| _____ | Have I placed my conclusion first to be considerate of my readers? |
| _____ | Is the organization consistent with the requirements of the genre? For instance, does my letter conform to my |

_____ readers' expectations regarding headings and arrangement of information?

_____ Have I achieved my purpose?

_____ Have I used design elements to make my document reader-considerate?

_____ Is my research solid? Have I verified all facts and statistics?

_____ Have I double-checked all math and other calculations?

_____ Are all visuals labeled? Are all the labels accurate?

_____ Have I placed all visuals in the best places in my document? Are all the visuals useful? Are they all integrated into the text by specific references?

_____ Have I given credit to all my sources?

_____ Do my conclusions logically follow from the analysis and discussion in the document?

## Sample Revising and Editing Checklist #2

_____ Have I checked all spelling, especially correctly spelled words that are not correct in context (such as "excepted" instead of "accepted")?

_____ Are my tenses consistent and logical?

_____ Do the nouns and verbs agree? Do the pronouns and antecedents agree?

_____ Is all the punctuation correct?

_____ Have I used capital letters correctly?

_____ Have I deleted any verbose words and phrases (such as replacing phrases such as "due to the fact that" with "because")?

_____ Have I used the correct level of diction for my audience?

_____ Have I corrected any dangling or misplaced modifiers?

_____ Have I used the active and passive voice correctly?

_____ Are the headings parallel?

Sample Revising and Editing Checklist #3

The following checklist incorporates the error it names in each entry. While this is amusing, it also helps you make sure that you understand each error. If you can't identify the error in the sentence, look it up in a reputable online or print source to make sure that you correct it in your own writing.

_____ Use your apostrophe's correctly. Omit the apostrophe when its not needed.

_____ Correct spelling is essentail.

_____ A writer must not shift your point of view.

_____ Of course, if any word is improper at the end of a sentence, a linking verb is.

_____ Prepositions are not words to end sentences with.

_____ Place pronouns as close as possible, especially in long sentences of 10 or more words, to their antecedents.

_____ One should NEVER generalize.

_____ Writing carefully, dangling participles must be avoided.

_____ Avoid clichés like the plague. They're old hat. So, go around the barn at high noon to avoid clichés and colloquialisms.

_____ Be more or less specific.

_____ And avoid starting sentences with a conjunction.

_____ Eschew ampersands & abbreviations, etc.

_____ Do not be redundant; do not use more words than necessary; eliminate the superfluous words and phrases and expressions from being used in your writing at all times, now in the present time as well as the time to come.

_____ Don't use commas, that are not necessary. Parenthetical words however should be enclosed in commas.

_____ Even if a mixed metaphor sings, it should be derailed. So, take the bull by the hand and avoid mixing metaphors.

_____ Avoid trendy locutions that sound flaky.

_____ Be careful to use the write homonym.

_____ Don't use no double negatives.

_____ About them sentence fragments.

_____ Verbs has to agree with their subjects.

_____ Between you and I, case is important.

_____ DO NOT use multiple exclamation points and all caps to EMPHASIZE a point!!!!!!!!

_____ Exaggeration is a billion times worse than understatement. Understatement is always the absolute best way to put forth earth-shaking ideas.

_____ Proofread your writing to see if you any words out.

## Writing in Teams

Sometimes professional documents are written in teams. In these situations, people plan, write, and revise documents as a group. If you are involved in a team writing project, it's easy to peer-review and edit. You can divide the tasks any way that members wish: some people can devote themselves totally to one part of the project, such as gathering information or editing. In these instances, the jobs are usually divided according to skill sets as much as inclination: the most skilled and confident writers are likely to do the drafting, for instance, while the most technically skilled team members would read for content, and so on. Other times, however, every team member participates in every part of the process. Each method has its advantages and disadvantages, so you will want to experiment with different allocations of tasks with each writing team.

The following chart summarizes some of the main advantages and disadvantages of writing in teams:

| Advantages of Team Writing | Disadvantages of Team Writing |
|---|---|
| Draws on strengths of each member. | Teams may not have the specific strengths and talents required for the project. |
| Divides the work so no one member is overburdened. | Team members may not pull their weight, leaving you with far more work than you would have had originally |
| Allocates responsibility and thus can relieve tension. | Can add to tension if members perceive allocation of tasks as unfair. |
| Writing can be more fun because you are sharing it. | Writing can be more difficult because of disagreements and difficulty scheduling group meetings. |
| May produce a higher-quality product, drawing on every-one's strengths. | May produce a lower-quality product, homogenizing the style and content to satisfy everyone and thus no one. |
| Saves time. | Wastes time. |

With team writing, it's especially critical that you and the team create a style sheet before drafting. Because the individual sections will be written by different writers who are apt to have different writing styles, a style guide helps create a unified style and thus reduces the time spent on revisions.

# CHAPTER 6

## Write Instructions

———◆·◆·◆———

**YOU MUST REMEMBER THIS**

Instructions are step-by-step directions for doing something, such as carrying out a process, operating a machine, repairing an item, or maintaining a system.

**ALL THE RIGHT MOVES**

To write clear instructions, be sure you understand the process fully, focus on your audience, and write each step as a command. Arrange your information in time order in lists, including any necessary definitions and warnings. Use visuals to illustrate the steps.

We all need to know how to do things: how to change a tire, how to get to a destination, how to cook a special dish, how to hook up that new printer . . . The list is endless. We look to our professionals to instruct us, but not everyone who can do things well can explain how to do them in a way that we can understand. As a result, people who can write instructions and directions well are very much in demand. It's no surprise that the ability to write concise, correct, and clear instructions and directions is one of the most important uses of professional writing. This chapter will teach you what you need to know to explain step-by-step processes in writing.

## Master the Process Yourself

Obviously, you need to understand the process completely before you can explain it to someone else. If you don't get it, how will your readers? You're the expert here, the professional.

How can you make sure that you really understand the process that you're describing to others? Here's my trick: I try my own directions before I publish them. I'm not unique in this. For instance, professional cookbook writers test their recipes over and over before they share them. That way, the writers can make sure that their recipes are easy to follow and produce the desired product—no fallen soufflés or overcooked stews!

## Focus on Your Audience

Effective instructions focus on audience perhaps more than any other type of professional writing. You must identify exactly what your audience already knows and what else they need to know in order to provide the level of knowledge they require. For instance, instructions for building a computer directed at computer technicians will require much less background than the same instructions aimed at computer novices. You can skip elementary steps for the professionals, but your direction will be useless (or worse, highly frustrating) for the novices unless you include plenty of background information and fundamental instruction.

Read the following set of instructions and identify the audience. Explain what details you used to pinpoint the audience and their level of knowledge.

> **Preventing Sunburn**
>
> Follow these instructons to help avoid painful and dangerous sunburns:
>
> • Limit sun exposure, especially between the hours of 11:00 to 3:00.
> • Wear protective clothing, including a hat with a wide brim.
>
> • Use sunscreen, Apply sunscreen 30 minutes before going outdoors. Reapply at least every 2 hours. Use water-resistant sunscreen with an SPF (sun protection factor) of 15 or higher. The SPF will be listed on the container.
>
> • Avoid the sun while using tetracycline antibiotics and over-the-counter pain relievers such as ibuprofen. These medications increase sensitivity to the sun.
>
> • Avoid the sun while wearing makeup that contains alpha hydroxy acids. These cosmetics also increase sun sensitivity and the possibility of sunburn.

The simple sentences, everyday words, and jargon-free details indicate that the audience consists of everyday people interested in protecting their skin. Notice that technical terms such as *SPF* are defined in parentheses. The audience is not comprised of experts (physicians such as dermatologists) or scientists.

## Write Instructions in a Specific Style

You've no doubt noticed from the examples thus far in this chapter that instructions follow a specific format. Let's explore this format now.

### Use Commands

Instructions and directions are *not* written as a story in a narrative form. Rather, they are written as a series of commands in the imperative voice. Each command is placed on its own line. Compare these two examples to see how they are the same and different:

## Document #1: Directions

You should travel .1 of a mile south on Hofstra Blvd. toward Hempstead Turnpike. Then you should turn left onto Hempstead Turnpike. Follow Hempstead Turnpike 3.4 miles to merge onto Meadowbrook Pkwy North toward Mineola. Next, you must travel 2 miles and merge onto Northern Pkwy West via the exit on the left toward New York. Then you travel 20 miles and merge onto I-495 West via exit 29A toward New York. You must keep right at the fork in the ramp. You have to turn slightly right onto the Queens Midtown Tunnel exit. Unless you want to get really lost, you have to turn left onto East 39th St. Then it is important that you turn right onto Madison Ave. You will end up at your destination, the Statue of Liberty.

## Document #2: Directions

1. Travel .1 mile south on Hofstra Blvd. toward Hempstead Turnpike.

2. Turn left onto Hempstead Turnpike. Follow Hempstead Turnpike 3.4 miles to merge onto Meadowbrook Pkwy North toward Mineola.

3. Travel 2 miles and merge onto Northern Pkwy West via the exit on the left toward New York.

4. Travel 20 miles and merge onto I-495 West via exit 29A toward New York.

5. Keep right at the fork in the ramp.

6. Turn slightly right onto Queens Midtown Tunnel exit.

7. Turn left onto East 39th St.

8. Turn right onto Madison Ave.

9. End at Statue of Liberty.

The documents contain the exact same information, yet the overall effect is very different. The first set of directions is wordy and difficult to follow. The second set, in contrast, is succinct and easy to read. That's because the first document is written in declarative sentences, not commands, while the second document is written in commands. Further, the first document is written as a paragraph; the second, as a series of steps, each on its own line. Which set of directions would you rather be following? The second set, of course. Any audience will agree—especially if they are lost!

### Use Steps

Framing your instructions as steps rather than as a narrative makes them easier to follow. However, limit the number of steps. Including more than ten to fifteen steps will discourage an average reader from attempting the process. If necessary, break the process into two or even three processes to avoid an overly long list.

Further, place each step or command on its own line, unless the steps are very easy and naturally go together. This arrangement of information often upsets my students because they think they have too many "paragraphs" when they write instructions. That's because they are used to writing narrative style. Remember: Instructions and directions are most often presented in lines, rarely in large blocks of type.

### Include Definitions

Be sure to define any difficult terms. What you choose to define depends entirely on your audience, of course.

### Be Concise

People who read instructions and directions are trying to accomplish a specific task. They will rarely pause to read a general overview or a complex explanation of a subject. To be considerate of your readers, use a succinct style. Include precisely what the reader must know in order to perform the desired task, deleting any unnecessary words and phrases. To accomplish this, move additional information into an appendix, note, or even a separate document.

### Include Cautionary Notes

We live in an age of litigation; people sue often and easily. But even more important than protecting yourself and your company from a lawsuit, you want to help people complete a desired task without injury. This often necessitates protecting them from themselves. Whether we're talking about the infamous dope who drove away from the McDonald's drive-in window with a cup of hot coffee on her lap and then was astonished when it spilled and burned her or the knuckleheads who copy what they see on "reality" television shows, make sure that your instructions include any necessary warnings. We don't need anyone using their toaster in the bathtub, for instance.

### Use the Active Voice

And while we're on the topic of sentence style, use the active voice rather than the passive voice with instructions and directions. That's because the passive voice is wordy and confusing when it comes to giving instructions. For example:

| Passive Voice (no-no) | Active Voice (yes-yes) |
|---|---|
| The red button should be pressed to stop the display temporarily. | Press the red button to stop the display temporarily. |
| The green button is then pushed to the far left. | Push the green button to the far left. |

## Arrange Information in a Specific Way

As you've no doubt surmised by now, instructions are arranged in a very precise way. Here are the guidelines:

### Open with an Introduction

Preface your instructions or directions with an introduction if you will be tracing the steps in a difficult process. Here's what to include in the introduction:

- A brief description of the specific tasks or procedure to follow
- What you will and will not include in the directions
- What your readers need to know to understand the process
- When these instructions should (or shouldn't) be used

Regardless of whether or not you include an introduction, always be sure to include a title. The title should describe the instructions precisely. Read the following instructions and decide why the introduction is so effective.

---

### Truth or Dare

The underlying rule when deciding whether a product is authentic or not is to ask yourself: "Does it sound too good to be true?" If it does, it probably isn't true.

If you're still not sure, check it out: "Look into it—before you put it in your body or on your skin," says Reynaldo Rodriguez, a compliance officer and health fraud coordinator for FDA's Dallas district office.

To check a product out, FDA health fraud coordinators suggest:
- Talk to a doctor or another health professional. "If it's an unproven or little-known treatment, always get a second opinion from a medical specialist," Rodriguez says.

- Talk to family members and friends. Legitimate medical practitioners should not discourage you from discussing medical treatments with others. Be wary of treatments offered by people who tell you to avoid talking to others because "it's a secret treatment or cure."

- Check with the Better Business Bureau or local attorneys generals' offices to see whether other consumers have lodged complaints about the product or the product's marketer.

- Check with the appropriate health professional group—for example, the American Heart Association, American Diabetes Association, or the National Arthritis Foundation if the products are promoted for heart disease, diabetes or arthritis. Many of these groups have local chapters that can provide you with various resource materials about your disease.

- Contact the FDA office closest to you. Look for the number and address in the blue pages of the phone book under U.S. Government, Health and Human Services, or go to the FDA Web site. FDA can tell you whether the agency has taken action against the product or its marketer. Your call also may alert FDA to a potentially illegal product and prevent others from falling victim to health fraud.*

This introduction is effective because it's specific as well as interesting. It tells exactly what the instructions will describe. It also serves to attract the reader's interest, a nice bonus. This makes it more likely the audience will read on.

*Source: Public Domain, http://www.fda.gov/fdac/features/1999/699 _fraud.html

*Follow Chronological Order*

Instructions and directions are written in chronological order, from the beginning of the process to the end.

- Use numbers or time-order words (first, second, third, fourth, next, last, finally, and so on) if the steps must be followed in a specific order. These are called *fixed-order steps*.

- Use bullets if the steps in the process can be followed in any order to get the desired result. These are called *variable-order steps*.

- Include bullets to set off details under the numbered steps. This breaks large blocks of copy into considerate text.

Don't mix instructions with concepts. Instead, present any necessary background information before the instructions.

The following set of instructions has clear chronological order. As you read this example, decide how the organization helps make the instructions so effective.

## Introduction

Your doctor* gave you a diagnosis that could change your life. This document can help you take the next steps.

Every person is different, of course, and every person's disease or condition will affect them differently. But research shows that after getting a diagnosis, many people have the same reaction.

### Five Basic Steps

**Step 1: Take the time you need.** Do not rush important decisions about your health. In most cases, you will have time to carefully examine your options and decide what is best for you.

**Step 2: Get the support you need.** Look for support from family and friends, people who are going through the same thing you are, and those who have "been there." They can help you cope with your situation and make informed decisions.

**Step 3: Talk with your doctor.** Good communication with your doctor can help you feel more satisfied with the care you receive. Research shows it can even have a positive effect on things such as symptoms and pain. Getting a "second opinion" may help you feel more confident about your care.

**Step 4: Seek out information.** When learning about your health problem and its treatment, look for information that is based on a careful review of the latest scientific findings published in medical journals.

**Step 5: Decide on a treatment plan.** Work with your doctor to decide on a treatment plan that best meets your needs.

As you take each step, remember this: Research shows that patients who are more involved in their health care tend to get better results and be more satisfied.

*Your medical care might come from a doctor, nurse, physician assistant, or another kind of clinician or health care practitioner. To keep it simple, in this document we use the term "doctor" to refer to any of these professionals with whom you might interact.

*Source: Public Domain, http://www.ahrq.gov/consumer/diaginfo.htm

## Use Visuals

Instructions use visuals more than any other type of professional writing. That's because of the old saying "One picture is worth a thousand words." Many times, visuals explain difficult instructions far more clearly and concisely than words ever could. Photographs, diagrams, and other drawings help your audience follow the process more easily.

Instructions include other types of visuals and formatting as well. These can include:

- Abbreviations
- Boldface
- Changes in fonts
- Dingbats (such as ✱)
- Headings
- Italics
- Numbers
- Symbols (such as %, $, &)

Every one of these formatting devices has the exact same goal: to make your instructions clearer. Thus, use fonts, boldface, and/or italics to set off major headings.

> Always give credit to your sources, and be sure to get written permission to use any visuals that are not in the public domain.

# Chapter 7

## Write Professional Letters

———•◆•———

**YOU MUST REMEMBER THIS**
Letters communicate relevant information arranged in a specific format for a targeted audience.

**ALL THE RIGHT MOVES**
Along with e-mail, letters are the workhorse of professional writing. In your professional letters, always maintain a business-like tone, convey your message clearly, and build goodwill.

L etters (along with their first cousins, e-mail) are the mainstay of any professional organization and any professional person. Letters come in a dazzling array of variety, too. Here are some of the most common types of professional letters:

| | |
|---|---|
| application letters | letters of complaint |
| cover letters | letters of inquiry |
| direct marketing letters | letters of intent |
| good news letters | references |
| introduction letters | rejection letters |
| invitation letters | thank you letters |

While no two kinds of professional letters are identical, they *do* share certain features besides their format.

Professional letters :
- Provide information the reader needs
- Are brief but clear
- Establish the relationship between the writer and reader at the beginning of the letter
- Include any necessary background
- Build a positive image of the writer and the writer's organization and create goodwill
- Establish a good relationship between the writer and reader
- Attempt to settle the issue to reduce the need for further correspondence on the matter
- State what action, if any, is required on the part of the reader
- Have a polite and formal tone
- Are always keyboarded, not handwritten

Since the meteoric rise of e-mail, why has the letter not only survived but also flourished? After all, sending email is so much easier. Tap, tap, click, and your message is off. With e-mail, you don't even need a stamp and an envelope!

Letters are important in professional situations because, unlike e-mail, they convey an air of formality and importance. Letters signify a closer relationship with the recipient than e-mail does; after all, you went to the trouble of writing a letter, not just dashing off an e-mail. This isn't to say that you don't craft all your emails with great care. It *is* to say that letters still carry the prestige that email doesn't. This special quality extends to personal as well as business situations.

Let's start with the format of a business letter.

## Format of a Professional Letter

Professional letters are single-spaced on 8 1/2 x 11 inch paper. Usually, the paper is official company letterhead. If you are self-employed or writing from home, you can easily create your own letterhead. Simply use one of the fonts available on your software package as you keyboard your name and address.

Traditionally, professional letters were written in one of three formats: *block style, modified block style,* and *semiblock style.* The differences among the three styles relate to paragraph indentations and the placement of headings and closings. The following chart explains these differences in format.

| Professional Letter Style | Description |
|---|---|
| Block style | All parts of the letter are placed flush left. |
| Modified block style | Place the heading in the upper right corner and the complimentary closing and signature in the lower right corner, parallel to the heading. Do *not* indent the paragraphs. |
| Semiblock style | Place the heading in the upper right corner and the complimentary closing and signature in the lower right corner, parallel to the heading. Indent the paragraphs. |

*Block Format*

The following chart describes the guidelines for the block style. Vary it as explained earlier if you want to use the modified block or semiblock style instead. In general, I recommend that you use the block style because it is the cleanest and most professional-looking style.

**Block Style**

| Element | Format |
| --- | --- |
| Date | Month (spelled out), day (followed by a comma), year |
| Inside address | The recipient's address; place two lines after the date |
| Salutation | Recipient's title, last name, colon (Dear Ms. Jones:) |
| Body | Short, single-spaced paragraphs stating the information. |
| Complimentary Closing | Capitalize the first word, conclude with a comma (Yours truly,) Insert two lines after the last line of the letter. |
| Signature | Sign your name in ink. Leave three lines of space after the complimentary closing for your signature. |
| Initials | If the letter is typed by someone other than the writer, insert the typist's initials below the typed name of the signatory. Capitalize the writer's initials; use lowercase for the typist's (LR:st or LR/st). |
| Enclosures | Add "Enclosures" or "Enc." to indicate that additional material is included with the letter. |
| Copies | List other recipients alphabetically or by rank, from most to least senior. |

Your software package comes with templates for business letters. In addition, you can download formats from the Internet. You may wish to use some of these formats because they format your letters automatically.

*Model Professional Letter in Block Format*

Below is a sample informational business letter to use as a model when you write your own professional letters. The sidebars point out the key features of an effective business letter as listed earlier in this chapter.

---

**Council for the Promotion of Reading**
817 Sweet Hollow Road
Stony Brook, LI 17918

January 20, 2008

Mr. Tammy Dorenz
45 Anywhere Road
Anytown, Anyplace 11771

Dear Ms. Dorenz:

Most important information first; tone builds goodwill.

It is with great pleasure that we invite you to participate as a reader at Step's 20th annual Long Island Family Reading Fun Fest at the Rocky Point University Student Center in Rocky Point, New York, to be held Saturday, September 18th from 10 am to 4 PM.

Meets the reader's needs.

This event is cosponsored by the Council for the Promotion of Reading in conjunction with Rocky Point University and a number of Long Island's public libraries, literacy organizations, and educational institutions. The goal of the event is to celebrate reading as a fun, enlightening, and enjoyable activity for the entire family.

Cements the relationship between reader and writer.

This day of family literacy will include authors and celebrities reading to children and their families, literacy-based entertainment, hands-on arts and crafts, learning workshops, and more. A book fair will provide opportunities for parents and children to speak with authors and to purchase books. Complimentary refreshments will be available in our author's booth.

### Gives a good impression of the organization and event.

Last year the event was a success with more than 3,500 adults and children attending. Because of last year's achievement, we anticipate an even larger audience this year.

### Meets the reader's needs by providing information.

If you are available to participate, please think about the book(s) you would like to read, the approximate age groups you would like to address, and the times you would like to present. We are inviting you to read for approximately 20-25 minutes. Times available are 11:00 AM, 12:00 PM, 1:00 PM, 2:00 PM, and 3:00 PM. In addition, we offer authors a free exhibit table, giving you an opportunity to sell your book(s).

### Tone builds goodwill; provides needed information.

Thank you for helping us promote literacy to children and families across Long Island. RSVP to Harvey Wattle at 631-444-5561 or Harvey_Wattle@step.org. We look forward to having you share in our celebration of reading and literacy on Long Island.

Sincerely,

*Harvey Wattle*

Harvey Wattle
Author/Entertainment Committee Chairperson

Cc: Lidie Chin, Rocky Point University
     J.K. Ruiz, King's County Library Association

## Good-News Messages

If it's your lucky day, you'll have good news to deliver to your readers via a letter.

### Guidelines for a Good News Letter

Follow these suggestions as you frame professional letters that convey welcome news:

1. *Begin with the good news.*

   Opening with the good news not only delivers the primary message but also pleases your audience. This builds good-will for you and any organization that you represent.

2. *Provide details about the good news.*

   Include background and any necessary clarification. Don't repeat details that you've already given, because this wastes your readers' time and annoys them. Instead, answer any questions that your readers are likely to have.

   Present the details in order of importance, from most important to least important.

3. *Provide a positive closing.*

   By shifting your emphasis from the message to the reader, you convey the impression that you care about the reader. Your primary concern, you are suggesting, is to provide top-notch customer service.

### Model Good-News Professional Letter

The following is a sample good-news letter to use as a model. The sidebars point out the key features of an effective good-news letter as you just read.

**Hudson University**
101 Crispin Blvd.
Glassy Point, Idaho 75617

S.P. Goldstein, President

October 25, 2007

Ephraim McClain, M.D.
901 East 9$^{th}$ Street
Mountain View, Idaho 71891

Dear Dr. McClain:

### Good news is in the first paragraph

As you know, Hudson University will be celebrating Reunion Weekend on October 6-8, 2008. During this year's celebration, you will be marking the 25$^{th}$ anniversary of your graduation and the 100$^{th}$ anniversary of the founding of Hudson University. On behalf of the university and your fellow classmates, we enthusiastically accept your gracious offer to serve as the Reunion Chairperson for the Class of 1983.

### Details about the good news

As Reunion Chairperson, you will be spearheading the most exciting reunion Events of the weekend. These include the traditional candlelight parade through the village of Glassy Point on Friday evening, with you serving as Grand Marshall. You'll open the Grand Ball Saturday night, too. In addition, you will usher your classmates on the field for the half-time celebration at the Homecoming Game on Sunday. The Office for Development and Alumni Affairs will assist and support you in the planning and implementation necessary to make your reunion a great success. Your leadership in this capacity is integral to the success of Reunion Weekend. I'm sure you are as excited about this landmark celebration as we are.

### Positive closing

Thank you again for accepting this position. I have asked Associate Provost Lincoln Deerfield to follow up with you. We are honored by your participation at this leadership level. If you have any questions before then, please feel free to contact Lincoln at 716 555-5555.

I look forward to seeing you at Reunion Weekend 2008, if not before.

Sincerely,

*S. P. Goldstein*

S.P. Goldstein, President

## Bad-News Messages

If it's not your lucky day, you will have negative news to deliver to your readers via a letter. Bad news is rarely welcome, but it's inevitable that as a professional you'll have to deliver less-than-welcome news some of the time. Fortunately, there is an effective way to construct your letters so you deliver the message and the recipient doesn't shoot the messenger.

### *Guidelines for a Bad-News Letter*
Follow these suggestions as you frame professional letters that convey not-so-welcome news:

1. *Begin with a buffer.*

   A *buffer* is a neutral or positive statement that allows you to buffer—delay—the bad news. A buffer makes your reader more receptive to your message and thus less likely to stop reading. Here are two model buffers:

   - Starting Thursday, May 1, you will have access to your money 24 hours a day, 7 days a week, at Lightower Bank. [This buffers the closing of branches.]

   - Enclosed is the new parking sticker for your car. You may pick up two additional parking stickers in the office, as needed. Please remove any parking stickers you already have on your car. [This buffers an increase in parking fees.]

2. *Describe the bad news and provide details about it.*

   If you have a reason that your readers will accept, start with it. This helps prepare your readers to accept the bad news that you must deliver.

   Present specific, convincing details. Emphasize what something *is* rather than what it *is not*. Emphasize what the firm or product *can* and *will* do rather than what it *cannot* do.

   Always use a professional, polite tone. No matter how rude a letter or phone call you may have received from a customer, client, or community member, always maintain your cool. Never insult someone in a professional letter, no matter how idiotically the person acts.

   Don't hammer home the bad news, but make sure that your readers clearly understand the message. If you soft-peddle it too much, your readers might misunderstand your point. Then you'll be stuck writing a second letter and saying no all over again! Here are two model bad-news messages. They would follow the buffers shown previously.

- After careful consideration, Lightower Bank has decided to close 12 of its branches on May 1, including the branch office on 28 Weathervane Plaza. This will result in significant savings and allow us to serve you more efficiently.

- As of January 1, parking fees will now be $100 per car. This is a change from the previous fee of $75 per car. The new fee structure allows management to repave the parking lot, add a booth to shelter the attendant during inclement weather, and upgrade the facilities.

3. *Present a compromise or an alternative, if one is available.*

   Perhaps you have a way to satisfy your readers and create a win-win situation. Even if they are not totally satisfied and they choose not to accept what you offer, the fact that you made the offer will win you valuable goodwill. Here is a sample:

- To thank you for your understanding as we undergo this transition, Lightower Bank will be giving all depositors free checking for six months.

4. *Provide a positive closing.*

   This is exactly the same as the close of the good-news letter. You want to focus on the reader, not yourself or your organization.

Omit the buffer if you think the reader will ignore the message or skim it and thus miss the main point. Also consider leaving off the buffer if you and the audience have strained relationships and the audience will see the buffer as your attempt to evade the truth.

## Model Bad-News Professional Letter

Below is a sample bad-news letter to use as a model when you write your own bad-news letters. The sidebars point out the key features of an effective bad-news letter.

In the following situation, the customer had neglected to follow the directions on the paint can, omitting the base coat and painting over raw wood. The paint went on smoothly and looked fine, but soon began to peel off. The customer demanded his money back.

---

**Richfield Home Décor, Inc.**
Smithaven Mall
Mawatah, VA 28441

September 14, 2007

Mr. Barry Hernandez
10 Plitt Street
Westville, VA 28019

Dear Mr. Hernandez:

### Opens with a buffer, a compliment.

Improving your home is a satisfying experience. Doing the work yourself gives you the satisfaction of a job well done and allows you to do everything just the way you want. Richfield Home Décor is always happy when another customer joins the ranks of the do-it-yourselfers. We are ready to offer the products and advice necessary for you to achieve a professional result.

### Description of bad news. Tone is professional and polite.

All our paints are guaranteed to provide a satisfactory finish when used according to our specifications. One of these specifications, described on the labels of our latex-base paint cans, is that latex paint be applied over a base coat of oil-based paint when used to cover unfinished wood. That's because unfinished wood absorbs paint. Using latex paint over unfinished wood causes the peeling you described in your letter dated September 12, 2007. An oil-based coat of paint seals the unfinished wood. Then a latex finish coat can be applied without peeling.

## Alternative option

We are sure you will be as pleased with your woodwork when a base coat of Richfield Home Décor oil-based paint is applied over raw wood. I have enclosed brochures with tips on how to achieve a professional finished product with all our paints.

## Positive closing

We appreciate your use of Richfield Home Décor products and wish you the best with all your refinishing projects. Please feel free to contact us if we can be of any additional help.

Sincerely,

*D. L. Hughes*

D. L. Hughes, Customer Relations

---

Notice how the writer uses the passive voice to avoid placing blame: "... *when a base coat of Richfield Home Décor oil-based paint is applied over raw wood.*" Here's the same sentence recast in the active voice: "... when you apply *a base coat of Richfield Home Décor oil-based paint over raw wood.*"

## Consider Your Writing Style

No doubt, the vast majority of your professional letters will be read and quickly tossed aside. Some might be shredded, others crumpled. A few will be saved as important records for professional matters such as legal proceedings. Nonetheless, you never know where your letters will end up and how many of them will be saved . . . and for how long.

Every time you write a professional letter, realize that it matters. It represents you, and often, an organization. But also assume that your letter will be saved and might even become part of history. As a result, pay close attention to the style as well as the form and content. Be sure that your letters are:

1. *Clear*
   Your message should be obvious. Readers should come away able to understand what you have written. They shouldn't have to reread confusing paragraphs or scratch their heads in confusion.

2. *Concise*
   Use just the words you need. Don't waste the reader's time with padding, filler, and extraneous verbiage.

3. *Correct*
   Proofread your letters to catch errors in grammar, spelling, punctuation, capitalization, and so on.

4. *Ethical*
   Obviously, always tell the truth. However, there are more subtle ways to obfuscate. Don't hide behind imprecise words, jargon, euphemisms, and abstract terms. Don't twist loaded terms—words with emotional overtones, such as *liberal, regime*, and *patriotic*. Also, avoid errors in logic that deliberately mislead readers.

George Orwell illustrated this point brilliantly and famously in his essay "Politics and the English Language." In the following excerpt, Orwell illustrates how unethical writers hide the truth: "Defenseless villages are bombarded from the air, the inhabitants driven out into the countryside, the cattle machine-gunned, the huts set on fire with incendiary bullets: this is called *pacification*. Millions of peasants are robbed of their farms and sent trudging along the roads with no more than they can carry: this is called *transfer of population* or *rectification of frontiers*. People are imprisoned for years without trial, or shot in the back of the neck or sent to die of scurvy in Arctic lumber camps: this is called *elimination of unreliable elements.*"

5. *Graceful and elegant*

Choose the precise words you need and arrange them in the best possible way to communicate with your audience. Take the extra time to make sure that your letters are written with style.

### Model Professional Letter

Aside from being one of our most revered and important presidents, Abraham Lincoln was also a master stylist. Below is one of his most famous letters. Horace Greeley, editor of an important New York newspaper, had accused Lincoln of lacking direction and resolve. The Civil War was raging and Lincoln had already drafted the Emancipation Proclamation, but had not yet issued it. As you read the following letter, note Lincoln's precision of language and his graceful style. Also note how he states the issue directly; there is no doubt that his primary concern is preservation of the Union.

Executive Mansion
Washington, August 22, 1862.
Hon. Horace Greeley

Dear Sir.

I have just read yours of the 19th. addressed to myself through the New-York Tribune. If there be in it any statements, or assumptions of fact, which I may know to be erroneous, I do not, now and here, controvert them. If there be in it any inferences which I may believe to be falsely drawn, I do not now and here, argue against them. If there be perceptable [sic] in it an impatient and dictatorial tone, I waive it in deference to an old friend, whose heart I have always supposed to be right.

As to the policy I "seem to be pursuing" as you say, I have not meant to leave any one in doubt.

I would save the Union. I would save it the shortest way under the Constitution. The sooner the national authority can be restored; the nearer the Union will be "the Union as it was." If there be those who would not save the Union, unless they could at the same time save slavery, I do not agree with them. If there be those who would not save the Union unless they could at the same time destroy slavery, I do not agree with them. My paramount object in this struggle is to save the Union, and is not either to save or to destroy slavery. If I could save the Union without freeing any slave I would do it, and if I could save it by freeing all the slaves I would do it; and if I could save it by freeing some and leaving others alone I would also do that. What I do about slavery, and the colored race, I do because I believe it helps to save the Union; and what I forbear, I forbear because I do not believe it would help to save the Union. I shall do less whenever I shall believe what I am doing hurts the cause, and I shall do more whenever I shall believe doing more will help the cause. I shall try to correct errors when shown to be errors; and I shall adopt new views so fast as they shall appear to be true views.

I have here stated my purpose according to my view of official duty; and I intend no modification of my oft-expressed personal wish that all men everywhere could be free.

Yours,
A. Lincoln

## Letters of Recommendation

There are many times when you will want someone to recommend you for a position or an honor. The correctly placed good word in writing can make all the difference in your getting that plum position. In exchange, you'll pass on the favor by recommending other people you know for jobs or awards. As you can tell, letters of recommendation are very significant documents in a person's life. Therefore, it's worth the time and trouble to get them just right.

*What to Include in a Letter of Recommendation*
Follow these guidelines to write effective letters of endorsement:

1. *Start with your overall evaluation of the candidate.*
   Begin with your overall recommendation. You might state this as "I highly recommend [name of applicant]" or "I give my highest recommendation to [name of applicant]," for instance.

2. *State your qualifications to recommend the person.*
   Explain how long you have known the person, and in what capacity. This establishes your credibility to attest to the person's character and achievements.

3. *Use specific examples.*
   To be effective, letters of recommendation must be specific. Vague statements such as "He was a good employee" or "She works hard" won't do the job. Use numbers, facts, examples, details, and anecdotes to prove your point.

   Some people think you should include some negative examples to make your letter more convincing. After all, no one is perfect. Others feel that negative comments weaken your letter and open you to potential lawsuits. The choice is yours, but I do not include negatives in my letters of recommendation.

4. *Close with your overall evaluation.*

Your close mirrors your opening. In addition, indicate whether you are willing to be contacted in person for additional information and if so, how you can be reached.

Letters of recommendation are persuasive messages. They aim to move someone to action or belief. They use appeals to ethics, emotion, and/or reason.

### When Not to Write a Letter of Recommendation

Don't write a letter of recommendation if you don't know the person well or feel that you can't, in good conscience, recommend him or her. Perhaps the person hasn't been such a good worker or such a good colleague. A weak letter is often worse than no letter at all, as you're damning with faint praise. It's the old advice your mama gave you: "If you can't say something nice, don't say anything at all." Instead of writing a weak or even damaging letter, tell the person directly that you can't write the letter.

Also, with the increase in litigation, some companies refuse to write letters of recommendation. These companies fear that if the letter in any way can be construed as libelous, they are open to a lawsuit. They will confirm only that the person did indeed work for the company, state the position(s) held, and verify the number of years of employment. Always check with the Human Resources department at your company when you are asked to write a letter of recommendation to make sure that you don't violate company policy. Of course, you can always write a letter as a private citizen, if you wish to do so.

Benjamin Disraeli, Queen Victoria's prime minister, was the master of the vague reply. His most famous reply was likely the one he made when someone forced a manuscript on him for his evaluation: "Thank you for your manuscript. I shall waste no time in reading it."

## Model Letter of Recommendation

As you read the following letter of recommendation, look for the specific details. Decide why they are so effective.

---

19 East 5th Street
Hamilton, AK 85104

June 6, 2007

Admissions Counselor
Land Grant University Admissions Office
Four Corners, AK 85910

Dear Admissions Counselor:

### Opens with overall assessment

It is with tremendous pleasure that I recommend Christopher for admission to your graduate school. I have been privileged to have Christopher as an employee for more than five years.

### States writer's qualification to evaluate the candidate

Christopher has been my employee at the Hillside Public Library since 2002, where I have been a trustee (an elected position) since 1984. As the most senior member of the Board, I am thus well qualified to assess Christopher's performance. I can say without reservation that he is one of the finest pages/assistants that we have ever had. Helpful but not unctuous, discreet but not unfriendly, warm but not pushy, Christopher is the model employee. For example, he recommends books and movies to me, a service we very much appreciate. He is also extremely skilled with computers, leading to his promotion to manager of the Audio/Visual department of the library. We all know that AV is a vital aspect of library work, now and in the future.

### Specific examples

Hands down, Christopher is the most popular page among the patrons as well as the employees. I knew all along he'd be the ideal employee;

after all, he was class president in high school and has held leadership positions at Land Grant University. I know from my friends there (including senior administration) that Christopher is admired for his intelligence, integrity, and hard work. It's no surprise that the student government chose Christopher to chair the Ethics and Conduct Committee of the Student Government Association.

As a result, my director and I are delighted that he has decided to pursue his career as a librarian/media specialist. We eagerly anticipate being able to hire him as a librarian trainee and know that he will quickly ascend the ranks—all the way to director.

### Closes with overall assessment

Christopher is a bright, hardworking young man. There are a lot of bright and hardworking young men. However, there are few bright, hardworking young men who are mature, responsible, and good. Christopher is a cut above and I give him my very highest recommendation. Please do not hesitate to contact me at the above address if you require any additional information.

Sincerely,

*Melvin Potwin, DDS*

Melvin Potwin, DDS

## Letters of Inquiry

The purpose of a letter of inquiry is just what you'd expect: to gather information. You'll likely be asking about an important or sensitive subject, something you want documented in writing. Why use a letter rather than e-mail? As you read in the beginning of this chapter, a letter conveys a level of formality that an e-mail doesn't.

*Guidelines for a Letter of Inquiry*
Follow these guidelines when you write a letter of inquiry:

1. *Clearly identify your subject and purpose.*
   This information belongs in your first paragraph, preferably in your first sentence.

2. *State your question clearly and concisely.*
   Try to limit your letters of inquiry to no more than three questions. More than that and you'll overwhelm your reader, reducing your chance of getting a response. Remember: A letter of inquiry asks a favor. Therefore, keep your message short and to the point.

3. *Thank readers for their attention to this matter.*
   Use a professional and courteous tone.

   Indicate how you want to be contacted (telephone, fax, email, return letter). Be very sure to provide contact information, including your name, address, e-mail, and telephone. If the matter is time sensitive, be sure to include a date by which you would like the information.

   You can use this format for letters of complaint as well.

*Model Letter of Inquiry*
As you read the following letter of inquiry, notice its brevity. This shows your consideration for your reader's time.

---

**Cutting Edge Pharmaceuticals**
9 Industrial Blvd.
Troy, New Hampshire 65101

October 30, 2007

Mr. Richard Illsworth, Director of Product Management
Excelsior Computers
910 Nonesuch Corners
Lenexa, KS 45180

Dear Mr. Illsworth:

### States subject and purpose

My team is planning a scientific expedition to the rainforest of the Amazon to study specific plants for possible use in pharmaceuticals. We need rugged laptop computers that will withstand the challenging conditions I anticipate encountering. I understand that your new 910D is the sturdiest laptop currently available. I would appreciate it if you could answer the following questions:

### States questions

1. At what range of temperatures is the laptop designed to function?
2. How waterproof is the laptop?
3. Does the laptop interface easily with GPS systems?

### Closes with thanks.

Thank you for addressing my questions. I would appreciate a response by November 30 because I must begin purchasing equipment by that date. Information can be sent to me at the above address or by phone at (888) 555-0118.

Sincerely,

*Sarah Lipsky*

Sarah Lipsky, Amazon specialist

To summarize, the more important the message, the client, and the situation, the more complete preparation you'll need to do. You don't want to ramble and not convey your point. You don't want to provide too little information—or too much. Always use the correct letter format as well.

# CHAPTER 8

## Construct Effective Résumés

———◆◆◆———

**YOU MUST REMEMBER THIS**
A résumé is a summary of your qualifications for a job. It is designed to get you an interview so prospective employers can determine whether or not you fit the position.

**ALL THE RIGHT MOVES**
Tailor each and every résumé to the specific job. When it comes to résumés, one size does NOT fit all.

Today, there's stiff competition for positions, and people who can communicate in writing often win out over those who can't. Knowing how to write a powerful professional résumé can help you get the interview and thus the job you want. You'll learn these skills in this chapter.

### Definition of a Résumé

First of all, what is a *résumé*? The word *résumé* comes from a French word meaning "summary." A résumé, therefore, is a persuasive summary of your qualifications for employment. It is traditionally accompanied by a *cover letter.* Employers use résumés and cover letters to decide whom to interview. An effective résumé and cover letter must be tailored to suit the employer's needs and your qualifications as closely as possible. For that reason, savvy people like you have many different versions of their résumé, one for each specific potential job. Here's how to make your résumé work for you.

As you write your résumé, emphasize:

- Things you have done that are *most* relevant to the position for which you are applying
- How you are superior to other candidates
- What *you* can do for the company, not what the company can do for you

Also:

- Be realistic.
- Be truthful.
- Use the layout to emphasize key points.
- Relate your experience to the job you seek.

Remember: A résumé is a type of persuasive writing. As a result, be as convincing as you can when you are writing your résumé because you are selling yourself and your skills. The prospective employer shouldn't have to struggle to decipher what you mean, find hidden information, and follow your career path.

## What Do You List on a Résumé?

There are practical as well as legal issues here. Some information *always* goes on a résumé; other information *never* goes on a résumé. Still other information is optional.

Here are the facts you *must* include:

- Name, address, phone number(s), e-mail address
- Education
- Relevant experience

Here are the facts you *can* include:

- Career objective
- Previous and current employment
- Promotions
- Foreign language and computer language proficiency
- Volunteer positions
- Education and course work
- Honors and achievements
- References

Here are the facts you *never* include:

- Age (unless this is a qualification for the job, such as the police force)
- Health (It is assumed that every candidate's health is excellent.)
- Religious affiliation
- Political affiliation
- Height and weight (unless this is a qualification for the job, such as the police force)
- Race or ethnicity
- Gender
- Sexual orientation
- Marital status (as in married, widowed, divorced, single)
- Information about children and/or pets

*Be Truthful*

I said it earlier in this chapter, but it is well worth saying again: you are expected to put your accomplishments in the best possible light, but *always* tell the truth. Background checks are a hot topic in personnel circles today. Experts say a decade of litigation has nervous employers turning more and more to professional background checkers, who report that caseloads are growing at 30 percent a year. Investigators find discrepancies or outright lies in about one-third of the résumés they check. Your résumé, in contrast, will be squeaky clean.

*Top Résumé Turn-offs*
Avoid these blunders when you craft your résumés:

| Turn off | Example |
|---|---|
| Poor formatting and exotic fonts | *John J. JobSeeker*<br>ANN APPLICANT |
| Unnecessary personal information | I'm a single white male.<br>I'm a Libra. |
| Buzzwords that obscure meaning | As the Director of Integral Operations, my mission involves convergences in delivering synergized solutions to my strategic customers. |
| Vague descriptions of achievements | "I increased widget sales."<br>Instead, say "I increased widget sales by 25 percent, which resulted in a $2 million profit." |
| Incomplete contact information | Some people actually forget to include their own names and telephone numbers! |
| Spelling and grammar mistakes | Arguably, the worst error is misspelling the name of the company or contact person. |

## General Résumé Guidelines

As I've emphasized repeatedly in this book, successful professional documents are carefully designed to appeal to a specific audience. Here are my top ten ways to make your résumés powerful and effective.

1. *Use the appropriate résumé format.*

   You can present your qualifications in different résumé formats, the most common two being a chronological format and a functional format. Each format presents your qualifications in a different way, so choose the format that will best help you get the job. In this chapter you'll learn about both formats as well as ways to decide which format to use in each situation.

2. *Emphasize the skills that apply to the job.*

   Include ONLY the information that will help you land this job—the information that your prospective employer will want to know. You can find this out (and you will) by researching the company and the job. Then relate each and every detail on your résumé to the job you seek.

   Just because you've done something doesn't mean that it applies to your current job search. For instance, say you want to be a Wall Street stockbroker. Having worked as a cashier in a food store to put yourself through college is nice, but isn't germane to the job. Your internship at Big Investment Bank is.

3. *Emphasize the skills that show your superiority to other applicants.*

   Include promotions, honors, awards, achievements, mastery of foreign languages, experience with computers—in short, all relevant information that shows why you are the best candidate for the position.

Usually, if you attended college, you leave information about your high school off your résumé. However, if you attended a prestigious high school that directly prepared you for the position you're seeking, include the name of the high school on your résumé. For instance, if you are applying to be a pilot and attended a special high school for aeronautics, list it.

4. *Emphasize the skills that are most recent.*

Be careful with outmoded skills, or skills that can be perceived as outmoded. For instance, the fact that you earned a degree in computer programming ten years ago isn't going to impress a prospective employer because the industry has changed so much in a decade. And alas, there is a bias against older people, so beware of listing information that marks you as an old fogey.

5. *List information in reverse chronological order.*

Arrange your information from most recent to least recent.

6. *Use the* "you" *approach.*

A résumé appears to be about you, but it's really about them—the prospective employer. Remember: You are selling yourself. The audience wants to know what you can give them. Thus, always tell how your qualifications will benefit the company. Never ask the employer what they can do for you; always tell the employer what you can do for them. Here's an example:

Ineffective Job Objective:

A position where I can gain experience in writing computer documents.

Effective Job Objective:

A position that allows me to use my background in computer science to write computer documentation.

7. *Try to limit your résumé to one page.*

This depends on your age and accomplishments, of course, but usually you can summarize what you've done in one page with a print résumé. If you do decide to add a second page, it should be at least half full or do not include it. Writing three or more pages if you are relatively young looks pretentious and suggests you're puffing and padding your achievements. You can write a longer résumé if you're submitting it online. More on that later.

8. *Use templates.*

As I've emphasized repeatedly, successful professional documents use design elements to make them easier to read. Software programs include templates for different documents. When you are just starting out or you haven't been in the workforce for some time, without too much effort you can format your material in a template to make it look attractive. Using templates also makes it easier to rearrange information as you tailor each résumé to each specific job application.

9. *Be concise.*

Without sacrificing content, try to be as succinct as possible. Here's an example:

Verbose:  Member, IEEE, 2003—2004
           Member, IEEE, 2004—2005
           Member, IEEE, 2005—2006
           President, IEEE, 2007—2008

Concise:  Member, IEEE, 2003—2006
           President, 2007—2008.

10. *Use action verbs.*

Describe your accomplishments and skills with action verbs rather than complete sentences because action verbs are forceful and concise. Following is an example (I underlined the action verbs):

- <u>Drafted</u> planting designs for commercial and residential projects
- <u>Figured</u> cost estimates for subcontractor bidding
- <u>Installed</u> landscape designs and plant materials

Refer to the following list of action verbs as you create your résumés:

| | | | |
|---|---|---|---|
| accomplish | demonstrate | inspect | qualify |
| achieve | design | install | raise |
| act | detail | institute | recommend |
| adapt | determine | instruct | reconcile |
| administer | develop | integrate | record |
| advertise | devise | interpret | recruit |
| advise | direct | interview | rectify |
| aid | distribute | introduce | redesign |
| analyze | draft | invent | reduce |
| apply | edit | investigate | regulate |
| approach | employ | lead | relate |
| approve | encourage | maintain | renew |
| arrange | enlarge | manage | reorganize |
| assemble | enlist | manipulate | report |
| assess | establish | market | represent |
| assign | estimate | mediate | research |
| assist | evaluate | moderate | resolve |
| attain | examine | modify | review |
| budget | exchange | monitor | revise |
| build | execute | motivate | scan |
| calculate | exhibit | negotiate | schedule |
| chair | expand | obtain | screen |
| clarify | expedite | operate | select |
| collaborate | facilitate | order | sell |
| communicate | familiarize | organize | serve |
| compare | forecast | originate | settle |

| | | | |
|---|---|---|---|
| compile | formulate | oversee | solve |
| complete | generate | perceive | speak |
| conceive | govern | perform | staff |
| conciliate | guide | persuade | standardize |
| conduct | handle | plan | stimulate |
| consult | head | prepare | summarize |
| contract | hire | present | supervise |
| control | identify | preside | support |
| cooperate | implement | process | survey |
| coordinate | improve | produce | synthesize |
| correct | increase | program | systematize |
| counsel | index | promote | teach |
| create | influence | propose | train |
| decide | inform | provide | transmit |
| define | initiate | publicize | update |
| delegate | innovate | publish | write |

## Chronological Résumés

A *chronological résumé* summarizes your accomplishments in reverse chronological order, starting with the most recent accomplishments and working backward. This type of résumé emphasizes degrees, job titles, and dates. It is the traditional type of résumé, the one that most people know.

### Advantages of a Chronological Résumé
Consider using a chronological résumé when:
- your education and experience are logical preparation for the job you want
- you have an impressive education and/or job history
- you have impressive honors and awards

## Sample Chronological Résumés

Following are two excellent examples of chronological résumés:

---

### Julia Ann Deerfield
**17 Main Street**
**Clover City, CA 890271**
**Cell: 918–555–5574**
**JuliaDeerfield@gmail.com**

**EXPERIENCE:** | **SAN MATEO INSTITUTE OF TECHNOLOGY**    San Mateo, CA
| Assistant-Associate Dean    2005—Present

- Provide administrative support to the associate Dean of Graduate Studies. Schedule appointments, meetings, and travel arrangements
- Create reports, letters, and interoffice memos
- Assist with the compiling of the yearly budget
- Maintain and file vendor invoices
- Assist with special projects

**J.P. MORGAN CHASE**    Tempe, AZ
**Team Leader—Customer Service**    1999—2004

- Used strong communication skills to provide training on all new products, materials, and procedure updates to ensure departmental compliance
- Coached new and seasoned employees with e-mail and phone quality
- Conducted employee reviews to develop action plans to improve performance
- Met or exceeded monthly goals regarding accuracy in processing, handling customer issues, and providing appropriate resolution
- Accepted overtime assignments dependably and reliably
- Used the Internet and Microsoft Office software to compile daily reports and perform general clerical duties

**EDUCATION:**    San Mateo State College    San Mateo, CA
Bachelor of Science in Management
Technology    August 2007

**SKILLS:**    Word, Excel, PowerPoint, Access, Lotus Notes, Visual Basic, Outlook, KANA and Oracle

**LANGUAGES:**    Fluent in spoken and written Spanish

# JOHN DOE

123 Main Street, Anytown, NY 12345

(631) 456-7890   (631) 987-6543   john.doe@myemailaddress.com

| **Summary of Qualifications:** | • Possesses ten years of progressive experience in software, computing and network engineering with an emphasis on solving complex product development problems.<br>• Highly effective both as a leader and a follower.<br>• Employs an unwavering work ethic with the proven ability to deliver results in a high-pressure, deadline driven environment. |
|---|---|

| **Objective:** | To obtain a position in which I can provide direct contributions to the success of the organization. |
|---|---|

| **Key Skils:** | **TECHNICAL**<br>• Database Administration<br>• Database Programming<br>• Web Administration<br>• Web Programming<br>• Network Administration<br>• Documentation | **MANAGERIAL**<br>• Project Management and Planning<br>• Supervision and Team Building<br>• Cost Analysis<br>• Client Relationship Management<br>• Mentoring and Training |
|---|---|---|

| **Experience:**<br><br>*"John's notable qualities include solid technical and problem solving skills, initiative to learn new technology and work independently, professionalism, and excellent training and communication skills."*<br>**- J. Smith Ebix.Com** | **Development Manager**          Winter 2000 - Present<br>Software Company, Inc. – Hauppauge, NY<br><br>**Responsibilities:**<br>Provide technical management and leadership of Computershare development initiatives. Mentor junior programmers, develop and maintain internal applications and databases.<br><br>**Accomplishments:**<br>• Developed and maintained mutual-fund proxy tabulation database and related software.<br>• Developed 3-Tier Web based reporting application using .Net Remoting, SOAP, SQL server 2000 and MSSQL Reporting Services.<br>• Developed and maintained electronic document delivery database and related web based consent collection software.<br>• Developed software to maintain and manage a 100-seat call center.<br>• Built multi-language, database driven on-line surveys for ACNielsen.<br>• Developed an inventory management system for internal mailing and fulfillment operation.<br>• Promoted to Development Manager in March 2005.<br>• Promoted to Lead Developer in 2002. |
|---|---|

| Experience Continued: | **Oracle/Web Administrator** Summer 1998 – Winter 2000 California Insurance Company – Walnut Creek, California |
|---|---|
| | **Responsibilities:** Maintain and develop the EBIX platform of insurance products. Provide web and database administration and third level escalated client support for the Ebix.Com suite of insurance applications. |
| | **Accomplishments:** |
| | • Named support engineer of the year for 1999. |
| | • Developed and implemented client knowledgebase and incident tracking website. |
| | • Created Ebix.com clustering and availability strategy. |
| | • Promoted to Oracle Administrator from Network Engineer |
| | **Field Network Consultant** Summer 1995 – Summer 1998 Custom Network Solutions, Inc. - Hauppauge, NY |
| | **Responsibilities**: Provide on-site network support for company clientele. |
| | **Accomplishments:** |
| | • Converted 300 node Netware 3.12 network to Windows NT 4.0 |
| | • Designed and configured Remote Access solution for MSC Industrial Supply. |
| | • Administered and maintained a 300 node network |

| **Technical Expertise** | **Programming** | **Database** |
|---|---|---|
| | • ASP.NET, Remoting.NET | • MS SQL Server 6.5/7.0/2000 |
| | • C#, C++ | • Oracle 7.3/8i |
| | • ASP 3.0 | • Btrieve/Pervasive SQL |
| | • Web Services / SOAP | • Access |
| | • SQL Reporting Services | |
| | • HTML/XML/JavaScript | **Operating Systems** |
| | • T-SQL, PL/SQL | • Windows 95/98/NT/ME/XP |
| | • Stored Procedures / Triggers | • Windows NT Server 4.0/2000 |
| | • Crystal Reports 6.5/10 | • Active Directory |
| | • Website Layout | • Netware 3.12/4.11 |
| | • Graphic Design | |

| **Certifications /Education** | • Microsoft Certified Systems Engineer (MCSE) |
|---|---|
| | • Certified Oracle Database Administrator (OCP) |
| | • Certified Netware Engineer (CNE) |
| | • A+ Certification |
| | • Senior Status at the State University of New York at Farmingdale (4.0 GPA) |

References and Recommendations Available Upon Request

## Skills Résumés

A *skills résumé* (also called a *functional résumé*) emphasizes your skills—the tasks you can perform. Consider using a skills résumé in the following situations:

- You wish to conceal your age if you are older. (Regrettably, there is often a bias against more mature and experienced workers.)

- Your education and experience are not the usual preparation for the job you want.

- Your skills are more impressive than your job titles or length of experience.

- Arranging your recent work history in reverse chronological order would create the wrong impression (perhaps because you have been demoted, fired, or you hopped from job to job).

- You are a nontraditional applicant with little paid work experience but lots of volunteer experience.

- You have recently changed career goals.

- You want to show that you have taken the time to analyze your capabilities and their relevance to the position you are seeking as well as to market your strongest attributes.

The skills you list on your skills résumé do not necessarily have to be the result of employment. Course assignments and volunteer work often provide valuable skills that  transfer well to paid work.

## Advantages of a Skills Résumé

Since developing a successful skills résumé means that you have analyzed yourself and the company's requirements in depth, a skills résumé demonstrates your analytical ability as well as your job skills.

A skills résumé also helps prospective employers find your talents quickly. That's because they don't have to wade through a list organized by dates or position titles to figure out whether or not you have the skills they need.

## How to Create a Skills Résumé

If you decide to create a skills résumé, choose three or four of your strongest skills—the ones that best suit the position for which you are applying. Arrange all your experience under these categories. Then look at the jobs you have held, the classes you have taken, and the volunteer positions you've had. See which positions show how you have best used these skills. Last, arrange the skills and the details under them from most to least important.

If you are a middle-aged candidate with a great deal of experience, I strongly suggest that you consider including only the last ten years of your work/volunteer experience. Never lie, but don't parade your age. Once you get your foot in the door at the interview, you can share as much of your job history as necessary, or as you wish.

## Sample Skills Résumés

Following are two excellent examples of skills résumés:

# TINA ZEMBROSKI

## OBJECTIVE

A career in industrial management, beginning with product supervision.

## SKILLS

**Organization**

- Served as Editor-in-Chief of the college yearbook, administering a $60,000 budget and a staff of 15 students.
- Coordinated Reunions Weekend for the Alumni Office: 40,000 people attended.
- Organized and directed the Winter Workshops for the College Council.

**Written and Oral Communication**

- Trained staff of 53 people for Autism Phon-a-Thon, raising $200,000.
- Served as anchorperson for college radio station during senior year.
- Interfaced with staff, parents, and students as a senior RA for two years.

**Research**

- Graduated with "Distinction" as a result of my senior honors thesis
- Worked as a library page for two years in the Reference Department
- Investigated information for radio station reportage.

## EDUCATION

2004-2008     City College                                    Any City, TX
B.A., Business Administration and Computer Science
Graduated summa cum laude

FAX (123) 098-7654 • E-MAIL ME@MYCOMPANY.COM
12345 MAIN STREET • ANY CITY, STATE OR PROVINCE 12345-6789
PHONE (123) 456-7890

# R. J. D'Amboise
**39 Carman Street, Apt.2 B**
**Meadville, PA 71890**
**Phone: (317) 555-5555**
**Email: RJD'Amboise@gmail.com**

## OBJECTIVE
Trained, dependable, enthusiastic worker seeking a management position in the hospitality industry.

## SUMMARY OF QUALIFICATIONS
**Supervision**
- Supervise shifts and direct 30 employees
- Train employees in developing effective customer service

**Operations Management**
- Control food, beverage, and labor costs by adjusting crew labor according to sales trends and inventory
- Recruit and hire employees; schedule employees within labor constraints
- Develop action plans to achieve goals and objectives for cost containment and employee retention

**Customer Service**
- Ensure high-quality, consistent customer satisfaction through communication
- Negotiate and resolve conflicts promptly and satisfactorily
- Awarded "5 Star Service Award" 2006, 2007

## SUMMARY OF EXPERIENCE
**Pasta Cuchina**                        Meadville, PA                        2005-present
Crew Member, 2005; Crew Leader, 2006; Manager, 2007-present

## EDUCATION
**University of Nevada- Las Vegas**   *B. S. Hospitality and Tourism*   2004
Chancellor's Award for Academic Excellence
Maitre d'hotel Gold Hat Award for Outstanding Achievement

**References available upon request**

A CV is a curriculum vitae. It's an uber-résumé used by people applying for academic positions. Unlike conventional résumés, a CV can (and often does) run twenty-plus pages.

## Résumé Formats

Traditionally, résumés and cover letters were print documents prepared on good-quality white or beige bond paper. They were folded, placed in envelopes, and mailed to prospective employers. Increasingly, however, résumés and cover letters are transmitted electronically. This entails different formatting methods.

Following are the four different formats:

1. *A print version.*
   This is the traditional format described above. It contains bulleted lists, italicized text, bold text, and other elements of professional writing.

2. *A scannable version.*
   This format contains the same information but none of the bullets, italics, bold text, and other elements of professional writing.

3. *A plain text version.*
   This is a plain text file ready to copy and paste into online forms or post in online résumé databases. This is also referred to as an ASCII copy.

4. *An e-mail version.*
   This is another plain text copy, but it is formatted for the length-of-line restrictions in e-mail. This is also an ASCII copy.

   For example, the city of Toronto uses a Human Skills Management System called "Resumix" to manage resumes. Thanks to the latest technology, your résumé will be scanned into a computer system as an image. The system looks at the image to distinguish every letter and number and creates a text file. Then artificial intelligence "reads" the text and extracts important information from the résumé, such as your name, address, phone number, work history, years of experience, education, and skills.

*The résumé you post online or scan is the same document that you created to print out and mail or hand to prospective employers or hand to interviewers.* You <u>do not</u> create a new résumé. You <u>do</u> change the format of your résumé to make it easy for you to post, copy and paste, or e-mail it to employers. Computer software can extract skills from many résumé formats. Computer software can also read a hybrid of résumé formats.

## *Tips for Maximizing "Hits"*

- Use as many of the key words as possible to define your skills, experience, education, professional affiliations, etc.

- Increase your list of key words by including specifics. For example, list the names of software you use, such as Microsoft Word and Lotus 1-2-3.

- Describe your experience with concrete words rather than vague descriptions. For example, it is better to use "managed a team of 15 software engineers" than "responsible for managing, training . . ."

- Be concise.

- Be truthful.

- Use more than two pages if necessary. The computer can easily handle multiple-page résumés, and it uses all of the information it extracts from your resume to determine if your skills match available positions. This allows you to provide more information than you would for a human reader.

- Use jargon and acronyms specific to your industry (spell out the acronyms for human readers).

- Use common headings such as *Objective, Experience, Education, Employment, Work History, Positions Held, Skills, Summary of Qualifications, Accomplishments, Certificates, Licenses, Affiliations, Languages,* etc.

Before you send your résumé to an employer, run a test by sending it to yourself and to a friend to see how it looks after going through the Internet. This will help you identify any additional formatting problems you need to correct before you start sending it out to possible employers.

Keywords are the most critical part of a scannable résumé because they are what the computer picks up and matches to the posting or advertisement. If you chose to include a job objective – and I strong suggest that you do—be very sure to include every single word listed in an online posting or print ad. Since many résumés are first vetted through a filter, your résumé be automatically rejected unless it has a sufficient number of the key words in the posting or ad.

## Five Final Points

There's a lot of information in this chapter, so let me end with five key points to remember:

1. Take the time to know the company or organization you are contacting.
2. Know what you have to offer. Analyze your strengths and weaknesses.
3. Be prepared to show the employer that you can do the job—and do it well.
4. If at all possible, target your résumé to an individual rather than a position.
5. Spend the time to get it right. You have no chance of getting an interview if your résumé contains errors.

# CHAPTER 9

## Create Professional Reports

———•◦•———

**YOU MUST REMEMBER THIS**

Reports come in many different varieties, including papers, empirical research reports, proposals, progress reports, analytical reports, and policies.

**ALL THE RIGHT MOVES**

Despite their differences, all reports contain a number of standard elements designed to help readers find the information they need.

A *report* is any written document describing the findings of some individual or group. I'll bet you're thinking: "That's a pretty big definition," and you would be correct. That's because professional reports come in many different varieties, depending on the needs of your audience.

Before you can write any professional reports, you have to know what types are available to you. This chapter provides an overview of some of the major types of reports and instructions for writing them. I've also included models, so you can gauge the style, tone, and content of each type.

## White Papers

Perhaps you've heard on the news: "The XYZ Agency has just issued a white paper on this hot-button topic." I'll bet you have, because every day, agencies, organizations, governments, and individuals issue white papers on a wide variety of topics. Technically, a *white paper* is a government report, bound in white. However, as you read in chapter 5, the term "white paper" has come to be used for any informative report that is circulated to pass along information. Often, a white paper is designed to bring about change. To do so, the white paper states an organization's position or philosophy about a social issue, political situation, or other subject. The white paper may explain the results, conclusions, or construction resulting from a committee, research collaboration, or design and development effort.

While we are on the subject of papers, *a green paper* is a preliminary report of a government proposal. It is published in order to spark discussion. A *blue book* is a report published by the British government. (Yes, it is bound in blue.)

*How to Write a White Paper*
White papers can be any length, but they usually range from about four pages to about twenty-five pages, the average being about ten pages. The tone depends on the purpose, so the writer can be neutral or persuasive. Most white papers have illustrations to supplement the text. Nowadays, most white papers are posted on the Internet so the intended audience can download them. However, white papers can be distributed to people in person or through individual e-mails.

Following is a sample outline for a white paper. Vary the outline to accommodate your purpose and audience, of course.

I. Introduction
   A. Title
   B. Abstract (1- or 2- paragraph summary)
II. Background
   A. History of your group
   B. Your credentials
III. Need
   A. Describe the need for this white paper.
   B. Explain why the problem is significant and deserves
      attention.
IV. Solution
   A. Describe your solution(s) to the problem
   B. Describe how, when, and with what resources the
      solution(s) will occur.
   C. Include a time line of the project.
V. Benefits
   A. Describe how your solution will benefit the immediate
      audience.
   B. Describe how your solution will benefit others.

*Model White Paper*
Following is an excerpt from a white paper that Australia
issued in 2003. As you read this passage, notice how the
writers state the points clearly and directly.

---

**Australia's Place in the International System**

Throughout its history as an independent country, Australia has been
actively involved in international affairs both within and beyond the
Asia-Pacific region to which it belongs. This is a natural consequence
of the outward-looking nature of Australian society. We have strong
links and close affinities with Europe and North America, a long history
of active political, military and economic involvement in Asian affairs,
and a vibrant economy which is deeply enmeshed in the international
flow of trade and finance. Every year Australians make more than

three million visits overseas and we welcome to our country annually around five million foreign visitors. The security and prosperity of the Australian people depend vitally on the quality and strength of the political, defence and intelligence partnerships and the economic links that we are able to maintain around the world. Australia's values, its make-up as a society, the strength of our institutions and our diverse international links equip us well to succeed in a period of international uncertainty and economic globalisation. The overall framework for Australian foreign and trade policy is global, reflecting the wide spread of our interests and relationships. Some of our interests are defined by geography, others are not. Some of our major relationships are shifting in importance over time, others stay relatively constant.

## Australia's values

Australia is a liberal democracy with a proud commitment to political and economic freedom. That freedom is a foundation of our security and prosperity. We have a long tradition of working with other liberal democracies around the world to defend and promote it, thus helping to build a more prosperous and secure world for Australia. Securing the independence of East Timor and playing an important role in the war against terrorism are only the most recent examples of Australia's defence of its values in the world.

Australia's political institutions and traditions are responsive, robust and decentralised. Debate is vigorous, the media are genuinely free and active, and power and influence are widely dispersed. Our system of government is a strength for us as a nation and provides a basis for successful foreign and trade policies.

The policies by which the Government advances the national interest are shaped by, among other things, the values of the community. This is particularly so of the commitment - by government and the community—to racial equality and religious tolerance. Our attachment to tolerance strengthens our standing in the world and thus our ability to advocate our interests. It is of particular importance at a time when small, unrepresentative, sectarian groups, like al-Qaida and Jemaah Islamiyah, pervert religious ideals for terrorist ends.

Similarly, we place great importance on fairness. The rule of law and equality of opportunity are crucial to fairness, and these are practices that we work to encourage in the rest of the world, as well as in Australia. They are at the root of our attempts to improve human rights and prosperity throughout the world.*

## Empirical Reports

Sometimes, you will need to test some equipment and report your findings. Maybe your job calls for you to perform a scientific experiment and inform your superiors about the results. Or you might have to test an idea, and then tell everyone on the job or in the community group what you found. In each of these cases (and many more), you will need to write an empirical report.

Empirical reports explore a solution to a problem based on what you already know or have discovered. They propose a new solution to a process. They also justify your reasons for your solution. As you write, you test your idea and then decide whether or not your solution will work.

### *How to Write an Empirical Report*
The different sections of empirical reports relate to the different steps of the scientific method. Following is a basic structure:

I. Abstract
    A. Introduction
        1. Statement of problem
        2. Importance of problem

    B. Literature review
        1. What is known about the topic
        2. Summary of relevant research
        3. Purpose of your report

*Source: PUBLIC DOMAIN, http://www.dfat.gov.au/ani/

II. Method
    A. Materials used in the report
    B. Methods used in the report
        1. How the research was conducted
        2. Who was involved
        3. What measures were used

III. Results of the research

IV. Discussion of the results
    A. Interpretations
    B. Implications

V. Conclusion/Recommendations

VI. Bibliography

VII. Acknowledgements

*Model Empirical Report*

Below is an excerpt from an affirmative action report. This section is from Part 3: "Empirical Research on Affirmative Action and Anti-Discrimination." The numbers in parentheses indicate the reference sources, which would be listed in the bibliography.

---

### 2 Effect on Earnings

3.2.1 Anti-Discrimination Policy, the Minority-White Earnings Gap
The ratio of the average black workers' earnings to the average white workers' earnings increased significantly in the 1940s, increased slightly if at all in the 1950s, increased significantly between 1960 and the mid 1970s, and declined somewhat since the late 1970s. (13)

Hispanic men earn 81 percent of the wages earned by white men at the same education level. Hispanic women earn less than 65 percent of the income earned by white men with the same education level. (14)

There has not been an improvement in the employment-population rate of black workers relative to whites since the 1960s. If anything, there has been a deterioration in the relative employment-population rate. (15)

Education and work experience are the two most reliable predictors of a worker's earnings. Black workers historically have had much lower education than white workers. Adjusting for racial differences in education and work experience can account for about half of the wage gap between black men and white men, and about one-third of the gap between black women and white women. Additionally, holding constant differences in individuals' test scores leads to a further reduction in the black-white earnings gap. For example, in one study, in 1991, black males earned 29 percent less than white males without any adjustments, 15 percent less after adjusting for education and experience, and 9 percent less after additionally adjusting for test scores. For women, the gap declines from 14 percent to almost zero after making these adjustments. (16)

There is some controversy as to how to interpret the black-white wage gap after holding constant differences in education, test scores, and other variables. In particular, differences in education or test scores may themselves represent the discrimination. Thus, the reduction in the racial gap after controlling for these factors may not mean that discrimination is any less, but it may mean that attention should also focus on discrimination prior to entry into the labor market.

Historically there have been great differences in the quality of education between black and white students. In South Carolina in 1920, for example, black students attended schools with class sizes twice those of white schools. Partly as a result of the Civil Rights Act of 1964, the Elementary and Secondary Education Act of 1965, and the Green decision, schools became increasingly integrated in the late 1960s.

The improvement in the quality and quantity of education of black workers since the 1960s accounts for about 20 percent of the gain in black workers' relative earnings. (17)

There is near-unanimous consensus among economists that the government antidiscrimination programs beginning in 1964 contributed to the improved income of African Americans. Nevertheless, it is difficult to draw conclusions about which specific anti-discrimination programs were most effective. And it may well be that the programs collectively helped even though no single program was overwhelmingly effective. (18)

## Proposals

A *proposal* is an offer to provide a service or a product to someone in exchange for money. Often, people and companies submit proposals to federal, state, city, or local agencies offering to do the best work for the lowest price. In these writing situations, the proposal process usually starts when a group that must address a specific need decides to seek outside help. When an organization sends out a description of work it needs done, the document is usually called a *request for a proposal,* or *RFP,* for short. In addition, teachers and scholars may submit proposals to get grant money for research projects.

### How to Write a Proposal

Of course, you will always present yourself and your product, service, or company truthfully and ethically. For example, an architectural firm gave a misleading proposal to a client. The firm charged not only for the hours of work devoted to the project (as the client had assumed) but also for the initial consultation, the time involved traveling to and from the meeting site, and the time spent reading background materials provided by the client. The total bill was twice what the client had anticipated. Now, some of these charges may be industry standard, but the client had no way of knowing that. As a result, the client was left feeling cheated.

The client paid the bill, but never hired the firm again and refused to recommend the firm to anyone. Further, the client told everyone about the misleading proposal. The secret to successful proposals and successful business dealings is no secret at all: clear, honest, and complete proposals. No hidden charges or nasty secrets popping up!

Proposals have the following standard sections, arranged as shown here. Notice that the summary is placed first, not last as you would expect. By placing the summary first, you are helping your audience locate the key information quickly. It is a good bet that unless your summary provides the information your audience requires, he or she will not continue reading.

I. Project summary

II. Project description
    A. Introduction
    B. Rationale and significance
    C. Work plan
    D. Facilities and equipment

III. Personnel

IV. Cost proposal (budget)

V. Any necessary attachments

---

A *business plan* is very similar to a proposal, except instead of doing a specific project, a business plan lays out the plan to start or expand a business. For a business plan, use the organization of a proposal.

---

*Model Proposal*
Following is a sample proposal. As you read it, notice how the information is arranged in sections. Also notice what kind of information each section contains.

---

**III. Project description**

Neighborhood Improvement Association, Inc. (NIA) is requesting a grant to strengthen the capacity of our organization by funding the anticipated two-year planning, development, implementation, start-up and expansion period for our new housing management company. Our successful joint-venture bid to manage 250 units of multi-family low-income homeownership housing, owned by the City, kicks off our expanded management program to attract working individuals and families back to an economically revitalizing area, and continue to stabilize and rebuild the economic base of this community.

However, our current organizational structure does not include the requisite separate housing management company prescribed by the City in order to be qualified to enter into municipal contracts to manage certain City-owned properties.

We will create a subsidiary housing management company structured to develop a public/private partnership tailored to meet the City's criteria.

We will then be able to contract with the City to manage a portion of the 2,500 occupied City-owned scattered-site substandard and inadequately maintained housing units in the community area we serve.

The new housing management company will also enable us to, independently and more effectively, manage the buildings that we currently own and manage. . . .

### IV. Personnel
NIA has a staff of 70: 10 professional, including 5 property managers; 10 clerical support staff, and 50 maintenance staff. Forty are full time, and 35 are part time. Our staff, board members, and many of our 3,500 housing residents provide volunteer work for our projects and community activities. Our Board of Directors serve on community boards, charities, churches and other community service organizations. In addition, NIA has fostered, built and maintained strong bonds and relationships with the community-based organizations of our community, as well as the City's housing agencies, to deliver a multiplicity of programs and services to the residents of this impoverished area.*

---

*Source: Public domain,
 http://www.npguides.org/guide/ grant1.htm
Alternate choice:
http://www.ocjs.state.oh.us/Funding/OCJS%20Sample%20Grant%20April%202003.pdf]

## Progress Reports

Many times as a member of a community group or an employee you will be asked to investigate a specific problem or situation. A *progress report* is a document that states how the work is going. Progress reports:

- Explain to the reader what has been accomplished and by whom
- Describe the status of the work performed
- Include any problems that have arisen and need attention
- Explain to the client how much money and time have been spent
- Detail what work remains to be done
- Enable the client to assess the work and plan for future work

As you would expect, progress reports are usually issued at regularly stated intervals to help head off potentially unpleasant surprises. Often, the organization that hired you to do the job will require a specific number of progress reports to make sure they are kept in the loop.

Progress reports are also called status reports.

*How to Write a Progress Report*
The structure of a progress report follows one of two basic plans. The opening and the conclusion are identical in both plans. Following are the two formats; choose the one that best fits your purpose and audience.

Structure #1

I. Introduction
   A. Project description
   B. Summary

II. Work completed
   A. Task 1
   B. Task 2
   C. Task 3, etc.

III. Work remaining

IV. Cost

V. Conclusion
   A. Overall appraisal of work completed to date
   B. Conclusion and recommendations


Structure #2

I. Introduction
   A. Project description
   B. Summary

II. Task 1
   A. Work completed
   B. Work remaining

III. Task 2
   A. Work completed
   B. Work remaining

IV. Task 3
   A. Work completed
   B. Work remaining
(continue for the number of tasks)

V. Cost

VI. Conclusion
   A. Overall appraisal of work completed to date
   B. Conclusion and recommendations

*Sample Progress Report*

A college student submitted this progress report. As you read it, notice what information it provides.

---

## Introduction

The purpose of this project is to research the effects that large woody debris (LWD) has on stream morphology through the formation of pools, sediment retention, and floodplain interactions. This progress report discusses the progress I have made from March 10 to April 17.

## Work Completed from February 1 to March 8

The previous progress report discussed the work that I completed for the proposal for this project. The information in my proposal included background information on the removal of LWD from stream, the effects that LWD has on aquatic species, and the implications that this will have for watershed and restoration managers.

## Work Completed from March 8 to April 17

During this period, I completed the first section of the report, which discusses the distribution of LWD within the watershed, and pool formation by LWD. The section on distribution notes how LWD is moved from a first order, narrow stream, where it is abundant, to a sixth order, wide stream, where only a few pieces can be found clumped along the banks. This section also provides a background for under-standing where pools will be formed by LWD within a watershed. The section on pool formations discusses the five main types of debris dams: dam jams, flow parallel jams, underflow jams, deflector jams, and beaver dams. I have also described the types of pools formed by each of these dams and their significance in stream morphology.

I also have begun working on the second section of this report, which will include habitat formation by LWD and its importance. The section of habitat formation discusses the importance of LWD for the endan-gered bull trout, macroinvertebrates, and periphyton (algae and diatoms) species. This section also notes how LWD affects other riparian plant species and the colonization of conifers on nurse logs.

## Work to be Completed by May 7

Next, I need to finish the section on habitat formation by making corrections and proofing the section. This will be completed by April 23rd. A section on the effects of LWD on stream temperature will also need to be completed, but it will only be a few paragraphs due to the lack of information available. I will then write the conclusion and management implications for the final paper. The entire project should be completed by the first week of May.

**Conclusion**
My research project is on schedule and I should encounter no problems finishing it on time. If you have any questions or concerns with this project, please feel free to contact me.

## Analytical Reports

*Analytical reports* focus on problem analysis. Rather than merely reporting data, however, analytical reports categorize the information and then investigate it in greater detail. From the analysis, the writer may evaluate the information, draw conclusions, and perhaps even recommend action based on the conclusions. Analytical reports can be further classified as follows:

- *Recommendation reports*
  In these reports, the writer advises a course of action.
- *Evaluation reports*
  Here, the writer emphasizes judgments. For instance, the writer might weigh matters relating to personnel, data, finances, or other situations.
- *Feasibility studies*
  In these studies, the writer analyzes a problem, presents possible situations, determines the criteria for assessing the solutions, holds up each solution against the criteria, and draws conclusions. In addition, the writer may recommend action.

The SEC requires all publicly traded companies to produce an annual report, which details the financial results for the past fiscal year. After an accredited accounting firm audits the results and certifies their accuracy, the annual report is distributed to all shareholders.

## *How to Write an Analytical Report*

Because analytical reports focus on analyzing problems, they often contain many parts. Notice that, once again, the conclusion is placed up-front in the report, not at the end. You have learned that this shows consideration for your readers because it helps save them time. Consider including some or all of the following divisions in your analytical reports:

I.   Abstract
II.  Background and Introduction
    A. Purpose of the report
    B. Why the report was written
    C. History of the issue; reason for the analysis
    D. Scope of the report (what issues will and will not be included)
    E. Procedure you will follow for analyzing (investigating) the topic
II.  Conclusion
III. Recommendations
IV.  Criteria for evaluation
V.   The information
VI.  Evaluation/Discussion

## *Sample Analytical Report*

The following excerpt comes from an analytical report prepared by the U.S. government. It concerns a geological survey. Notice the neutral tone and ample specific details.

U.S. Geological Survey Open-File Report 2007-1080

# Streamflow and Nutrient Fluxes of the Mississippi-Atchafalaya River Basin and Subbasins for the Period of Record Through 2005

By Brent T. Aulenbach, Herbert T. Buxton, William A. Battaglin, and Richard H. Coupe

## Abstract

U.S. Geological Survey has monitored streamflow and water quality systematically in the Mississippi-Atchafalaya River Basin (MARB) for more than five decades. This report provides streamflow and estimates of nutrient delivery (flux) to the Gulf of Mexico from both the Atchafalaya River and the main stem of the Mississippi River. This report provides streamflow and nutrient flux estimates for nine major subbasins of the Mississippi River. This report also provides streamflow and flux estimates for 21 selected subbasins of various sizes, hydrology, land use, and geographic location within the Basin. The information is provided at each station for the period for which sufficient water-quality data are available to make statistically based flux estimates (starting as early as water year1 1960 and going through water year 2005). Nutrient fluxes are estimated using the adjusted maximum likelihood estimate, a type of regression-model method; nutrient fluxes to the Gulf of Mexico also are estimated using the composite method. Regression models were calibrated using a 5-year moving calibration period; the model was used to estimate the last year of the calibration period. Nutrient flux estimates are provided for six water-quality constituents: dissolved nitrite plus nitrate, total organic nitrogen plus ammonia nitrogen (total Kjeldahl nitrogen), dissolved ammonia, total phosphorous, dissolved orthophosphate, and dissolved silica.

Additionally, the contribution of streamflow and net nutrient flux for five large subbasins comprising the MARB were determined from streamflow and nutrient fluxes from seven of the aforementioned major subbasins. These five large subbasins are: 1. Lower Mississippi, 2. Upper Mississippi, 3. Ohio/Tennessee, 4. Missouri, and 5. Arkansas/Red. . . .*

*Source: Public domain, http://toxics.usgs.gov/pubs/of-2007-1080/
Alternate model: http://www.census.gov/svsd/www/advtable.html

## Organizational Policies

*Policies* list and describe the rules and regulations for an organization. These reports describe the tasks an organization's members are expected to perform. As a result, policies serve the following functions:

- Describe appropriate actions
- Document required actions
- Help achieve uniform behavior
- Safeguard employees
- Protect organizations from litigation

Most organizations have policies on such issues as sick leave, retirement plans, personal days, travel, employee development, sexual harassment, and so on.

### How to Write an Organizational Policy

I strongly suggest that if you are asked to write an organizational policy, even for a small company, you give your draft to a lawyer for review. This way, you make sure that your policies are in accordance with all local, state, and federal laws.

If you are writing an organizational policy from the bottom up, it's usually easiest to start with a template. Locate policies from similar organizations to use as models. Compare and contrast them and see how they are similar and different. Determine which policies have sections that you *must* include and sections that you *wish* to include.

That said, organizational policies are commonly arranged as follows:

I. Introduction
    A. Name of the policy
    B. Statement of the policy
    B. Class of people are covered by the policy
    C. Policy's purpose

II.  General applications

III. Specific applications: detailed information about the main issues

V.  Attachments (forms)

*Sample Organizational Policy*

Policies and procedures are similar to instructions, but they go much further.

Here is an excerpt from an organizational policy used in colleges and universities:

---

The Family Educational Rights and Privacy Act (FERPA) affords students certain rights with respect to their education records. These rights are:

1. The right to inspect and review the student's education records within 45 days of the day the University receives a request for access. Students should submit to the registrar, dean, or head of the academic department (or appropriate official) written requests that identify the record(s) they wish to inspect. The University official will make arrangements for access and notify the student of the time and place where the records may be inspected. If the records are not maintained by the University official to whom the request was submitted, that official shall advise the student of the correct official to whom the request should be addressed.

2. The right to request the amendment of the student's education records that the student believes is accurate or misleading. Students should write the University official responsible for the record, clearly identify the part of the record they want changed, and specify why it is inaccurate or misleading. If the University decides not to amend the record as requested by the student, the University will notify the student of the decision and advise the student of his or her right to a hearing regarding the request for

amendment. Additional information regarding the hearing procedures will be provided to the student when notified of the right to a hearing.

3. The right to consent to disclosures of personally identifiable information contained in the student's education records, except to the extent that FERPA authorizes disclosure without consent. One exception, which permits disclosure without consent, is disclosure to school officials with legitimate educational interests. A school official is defined as a person employed by the University in an administrative, supervisory, academic, or support staff position (including law enforcement unit and health staff): a person or company with whom the University has contracted (such as an attorney, auditor, or collection agent): a person serving on the Board of Trustees; or assisting another school official in performing his or her tasks.

Upon request, the University discloses education records without consent to officials of another school in which a student seeks or intends to enroll. (NOTE: FERPA requires an institution to make a reasonable attempt to notify the student of the records request unless the institution states in its annual notification that it intends to forward records on request).

4. The right to file a complaint with the U.S. Department of Education concerning alleged failures by the University to comply with the requirements of FERPA.

Instructors cannot discuss a student's grades with his or her parents (or anyone else) unless you get written permission in writing from the student beforehand.

---

You can combine different types of reports to achieve your specific purpose, of course. In all your reports, be complete, correct, and direct. Make sure your audience has all the information they require ... but no more!

# CHAPTER 10

## Send Professional E-mail

---

**YOU MUST REMEMBER THIS**
E-mail (electronic mail) is the most common form of professional written communication today. The trend is not likely to reverse.

**ALL THE RIGHT MOVES**
Keep your emails brief and use the appropriate tone for your audience. Write clearly, concisely, and correctly.

---

Have you heard this joke?

> Lou books himself on a Caribbean cruise and has the time of his life—until the cruise ship sinks and he washes ashore on a deserted island. He barely manages to survive, subsisting on fish and coconuts.
>
> A year later, he is lying on the beach when the most gorgeous woman he has ever seen rows up to him. Shocked, he asks, "Where did you come from? How did you get here?"
>
> "I rowed from the other side of the island," she replies. "I landed here when my cruise ship sank."
>
> "Amazing," he says. "You were really lucky to have a rowboat wash up with you."

*"Oh, this?" she replies. "I made it myself, whittling the oars from gum tree branches, weaving the sides from palm branches, and assembling the bottom from eucalyptus wood."*

*"But, but, that's impossible," Lou says. "You don't have any tools. How did you manage?"*

*"Oh, that was no problem," replies the woman. "On the south side of the island, I found some strata of exposed alluvial rock. I simply fire it to a certain temperature in my kiln to melt it into forgeable ductile iron. I use the iron for tools and hardware." Lou is stunned.*

*"Let's row over to my place," she says. Her place turns out to be an exquisite bungalow, beautifully furnished. She offers Lou a pina colada from the rum she distills herself. Trying to hide his continued amazement, Lou accepts, and the woman excuses herself to freshen up. When she returns, she greets him wearing only strategically positioned flowers. She beckons him to sit down next to her. "We've been out here for a really long time," she purrs. "You've been lonely. There's something I'm sure you really feel like doing right now, something you've been longing for all these months. You know …" She stares into his eyes, invitingly.*

*He can't believe what he's hearing. "You mean—," he swallows excitedly, "I can check my e-mail from here?"*

Yes, ladies and gentlemen, we are all hooked on e-mail.

No one is sure exactly how much email is being sent, but everyone agrees that it is a lot—a whole lot. According to *Wired* magazine, business users alone sent an estimated 5-6 billion e-mail messages in 1993. That translates to the equivalent of 10,000 manuscripts the length of *War and Peace* each day. The *Los Angeles Times* put the number of yearly e-mails at 10 billion. The number reached 50 billion by 1997; 6 trillion by 2006.

As of 2006, more than 25 billion e-mail messages are sent *every day*. The typical e-mail user receives 600 e-mail messages per week (http://www.ferris.com/research-library/industry-statistics/).

It is plain to see that as a result of e-mail, we are doing more writing than we ever expected, and much of it is professional writing. Even people whose jobs never required writing skills find themselves writing a lot . . . of e-mail. According to conservative estimates, most business professionals spend between one-quarter and one-half of their time communicating through e-mail, including writing, reading, sorting, and sending e-mail messages. E-mail is far and away the most accepted form of written communication used in business. That's because it is fast, easy, and inexpensive.

Even if you are not working, you will need e-mail to communicate quickly and efficiently with many businesses. Some businesses, like eBay.com, communicate ONLY via e-mail: they have no telephone or U.S. mail communication with customers at all.

There is no question at all, then, that you will be writing a lot of professional e-mail. So let's explore how you can make your professional e-mail more powerful and effective.

## What Exactly is E-mail?

*E-mail* is an abbreviation for "electronic mail." The term can be written with or without the hyphen: email or e-mail. No matter how we write the word, e-mail is a way to write, store, send, and receive messages over computers.

Your blank e-mail page will look similar to this model, depending on which program you use:

| | |
|---|---|
| From: | Your e-mail address is automatically placed here. |
| To: | You insert your recipient's name here. |
| Subject: | You insert the subject of your e-mail here. This phrase is a succinct summary of the contents of your message. |
| Message space | |
| cc/bcc | |
| Attachments | You can attach a file to your message. The file can be a document or a visual such as a photograph, chart, or graph, for instance. |

- The "To" box is like the greeting at the top of a conventional letter, which is delivered according to the address on the outer envelope.
- The "From" information can be faked. This is how people send mass mailings as well as fake (often called "spoof") e-mails.
- There is usually a button to click to send a copy, labeled cc (carbon copy) or bcc (blind carbon copy). However, attaching some files can be dangerous. If the file has a virus, you will be infecting the recipient's

computer system. Some people won't open attached files and insist the information be embedded in the body of the e-mail.

Be considerate as well as professionally savvy by not e-mailing jokes to colleagues. At the very least, the jokes are a waste of time; at the very worst, they are potentially offensive and thus may open you to charges of sexual harassment. Further, some joke files have viruses, so you are not only running the risk of offending someone, you are also running the risk of infecting his or her computer with a virus. No joke is funny enough for these risks.

## The Ten Commandments of Professional E-mail

1. Use a professional-sounding e-mail address.
2. Fill in the subject box.
3. Provide sufficient context.
4. Be brief.
5. Use a considerate style.
6. Be clear and specific.
7. Be appropriate.
8. Use the correct tone.
9. Consider not responding.
10. Be correct.

Now we'll examine each commandment in detail.

### Use a Professional-Sounding E-mail Address

You must have an e-mail address to send and receive e-mail. When you send mail through the United States Postal Service, you don't have any choice about your name and return address: it is what it is. When you send e-mail, however, you get to choose your address. What's in a name? A great deal, it turns out, when it comes to sending professional e-mail.

Unless your profession involves participation in the adult entertainment industry, steer very clear of sexually suggestive e-mail addresses. Always.

### Avoid Idiotic E-mail Addresses

You just read that you can create any e-mail address that you want. Unfortunately, like tattoos, food consumption, and hairstyles, people tend to take their e-mail address choices to extremes. I have had students whose e-mail addresses were colorful and dopey, like *Fairyprincess, SheDevil, DaddysLittleGirl, SoccerFan, FreakyGurll,* and *StupidKid.* I've had students whose e-mail addresses were offensive, like *JuicyCutie, HotChick, Sxykittn, Bunsoflove69, Stuffmuffin,* and *DirtyMamma.* I've even had students whose e-mail addresses are nonsensical, such as *ChadtheLawnMowerGuy* from a young man who had nothing whatsoever to do with lawnmowers, lawn care, or even the outdoors. Why he chose this e-mail address I'll never know.

### Choose a Logical and Clear E-mail Address

Don't choose an e-mail name that is likely to be confused with another person, place, or thing. Avoid e-mail addresses that are apt to be misread or misunderstood, too.

So what *should* you choose as your e-mail address? Use your name, your real name. It's as simple as that.

Following are some ways to format your name on your e-mail address to set the tone for clear and professional communication. You can use dots, hyphens, or dashes, as the first example shows.

1. First name_ Last name @ domain name
   Laurie _ Rozakis @farmingdale.edu

2. First name.Last name @ domain name
   Jack.Larosa@gmail.com

3. Initials.Last Name @ domain name.
   CBulter@yahoo.com

4. Initials.Last Name.Professional affiliation@ domain name.
   GSmith.ieee@gmail.com

What can you do if you absolutely, positively, totally refuse to give up your silly e-mail address? Use the silly e-mail address in an account for personal email. Then open up a new e-mail account with a professional e-mail address to use solely for professional e-mail communication.

Remember: Your e-mail address can reveal a lot about your leisure activities, your age, and your lifestyle. Your e-mail address can give someone a false impression of your character before they even meet you. This colors the recipient's perception of the e-mail message you write, so always use a professional e-mail address for professional communication.

Regarding sending e-mail to others: In the past, many systems were case- sensitive. This means that you had to type upper case letters as upper case letters and lower case letters as lower case letters to make the address work. More and more, addresses are not case sensitive, but to be on the safe side and to make sure that your e-mail message isn't lost in cyberspace, always keyboard the address exactly as it appears on a document. It is easiest just to hit the Reply button or to use your online address book, of course, but you may not always be replying to a message or have the address stored in your online address book.

## 2. Fill in the Subject Box

Just because you send an e-mail doesn't obligate the recipient to open it and read it. You read earlier that people get a staggering amount of e-mail every day. People rarely have the time or inclination to read it all. How can you make sure that your message is read by the recipient? Use the subject box.

A study in the April 2006 issue of *Entrepreneur* magazine reveals that 43 percent of e-mail recipients open their email based on information in the subject lines. That means that close to half the people who receive e-mail use the subject line to decide whether or not to open the message.

Get both your message and your action into your subject line. State your point clearly in the subject line: to attend a meeting, to approve a budget, to accept a new policy, and so on.

Here are some examples of effective subject lines:

- Agenda for Tuesday's Department Meeting
- Shop Women's Early Fall Arrivals and Top-Rated Shoe Styles
- Summer Office Hours
- Simply Irresistible Winter Coat Sales

### Provide Sufficient Context

Your recipients aren't mind readers. And even if they are, they may not remember the last e-mail you sent. You know the one: it came in with the other six hundred e-mails the person received that day. As a result, it is vital to give your recipients the background they need to understand your message.

Include a brief summary of relevant information. You can:

- Quote the e-mail to which you are responding.
- Explain the situation briefly.
- Avoid pronouns that may be unclear. Use the nouns (names of people, places, things, and ideas) instead.

## Be Brief

I require my students to write detailed, descriptive, and discursive papers in the college English classes that I teach. These papers are invariably long. Very long. Some research papers approach 40 to 50 pages. My own papers were usually that long, and often longer. Not so with e-mail.

Ignore all you were taught in high school and college about writing a lot of text. E-mail is a different medium, a totally different kettle of fish. When you are writing e-mail, keep your messages short. After all, if your recipients want or need more information, they can always fire off an e-mail and ask you for it.

Try to keep your message to no more than one page, preferably no more than one to two paragraphs.

## Use a Considerate Style

A specific professional style has evolved for writing e-mail. It is very different from the style that you likely use with your other documents. That's because e-mail style is based on the special nature of the electronic medium.

Remember that your e-mail messages will appear in the message space, and that space is not very large. Further, some programs have type that doesn't automatically wrap from one line to the next, so your message might not appear the way that you keyboarded it. This is especially true if you write long sentences, which are apt to get cut and rearranged in odd ways. Finally, some e-mail programs automatically cut the message off at a set number of characters. This is surprisingly common, especially when it comes to sending e-mail to businesses through their own portals. Thus, you will be happily keyboarding away when suddenly no more letters appear in the message box. Then you know you have to go back and edit your message.

To conform to the unique needs of electronic communication, follow these three stylistic guidelines:

### Write Short Sentences

No more than fifteen words per sentence, no more than about seventy characters. The previous sentence is a great example because it contains thirteen words and sixty-seven characters. (And yes, I did count them!)

### Write short paragraphs

Figure no more than three sentences per paragraph. Breaking up blocks of type makes your e-mail message easier to read and thus more professional—just as you see with the text here.

### Consider Using Acronyms.

Since so many people send so much e-mail, they have developed their own jargon. These acronyms save time and space. Use these acronyms and expressions ONLY when you are 100% sure that your audience knows them and feels comfortable using them. They are very informal, so they are likely to annoy employees in a traditional and highly-structured company.

Following are some of the most common acronyms and expressions used in e-mail:

| Acronym/Expression | Meaning |
|---|---|
| BTW | By The Way |
| FYI | For Your Information |
| IMHO | In My Humble/Honest Opinion |
| RTFM | Read The Manual ("manual" here refers to any document) |
| LOL | [I] Laughed Out Loud [at what you wrote] |
| RSN | Real Soon Now |
| ROTFL | [I am] Rolling On The Floor Laughing [at what you wrote] |
| <g> | Grin |
| TTFN | Ta-Ta For Now |
| TIA | Thanks In Advance (also sometimes written advTHANKSance) |

An *acronym* is a word formed from the first letters of a phrase. Usually, all the letters are written as capitals. There are no periods between the letters, in contrast to abbreviations. For instance, OPEC is the acronym for the Organization of Petroleum Export Countries.

## Be Clear and Specific

Since you have neither time nor space to waste, state your message clearly and directly. For instance, if you want a product, service, or other consideration, ask for it directly. Don't make your audience read between the lines to tease out your message.

## Be Appropriate

You *can* write anything you want in an e-mail, but *should* you? No! Survey just a handful of people about ill-advised e-mails. I guarantee they will all know someone who was fired or even hauled into court over a reckless e-mail. Because it is so easy to push that Send button—and lamentably easy to send an e-mail to the wrong person—you must be extra careful about what you write—and to whom you write. Remember: Just because you intend the e-mail for one person and send it to only person doesn't mean that the recipient will keep it private. "Confidential" e-mails have a way of entering their own orbit in cyberspace, like rogue planets.

Following are some topics that NEVER belong in an email:

### *Negative Comments About Anyone in Your Company, Especially Management*

Even if you delete such a message, it can be retrieved and used in litigation. Further, e-mails with comments like this often get sent on, accidentally or intentionally. After a series of replies to an ongoing saga, someone forgets your sarcastic line buried at the bottom and forwards the e-mail to another colleague to answer a different question.

### *Criticism Regarding Peer or Staff Performance Issues*

If you say something foolish, you can always claim that your comment was misinterpreted; politicians do it all the time. But if you write something foolish in an e-mail, you are caught in the cross hairs.

### *Money Issues*

I have found that people will tell you details about their sex lives—astonishingly intimate details—before they will tell you about their pay. Further, if you are in management and you mention raises or bonuses, your e-mail can be used as proof that they were promised.

### Racial or Gender Slurs

Be sure to turn off the light and turn in your key on your way out the door. You are history if you commit this e-mail crime.

### Product or Service Liabilities.

Avoid any mention of these issues in an e-mail because competitors can subpoena your e-mails as evidence that you were aware of problems and ignored warnings.

### Competitor Untruths

Nothing like a good lawsuit, eh?

### Gossip About Colleagues

It is so tempting to pass on a juicy story or even happy news, but resist the pull to the Dark Side. Keep your lip zipped and your fingers away from the keyboard when it comes to sharing other people's business.

### Personal Details from Your Life

You think people care about your children, your partner, your pooch? They don't. Keep your private life private. The impression that work is One Big Happy Family is wrong. Work is Work. Family is Family.

### Certain Social Communication

E-mail is great for a quick note, for being efficient, for keeping people in the loop, for passing on important information, for creating a file you can search—but it is not always the best way to communicate. Despite the ubiquitousness of e-mail, there are times when a handwritten note or a phone call is far preferable. In these instances, sending a handwritten note or calling is considerate, better business, and socially correct. For instance, a condolence card should always be handwritten. If the family is close, you would call and/or visit as well as write, of course.

What's left? Professional e-mail. Now you've got it!

*Tone* is the writer's attitude toward the subject matter and audience.

## Use the Correct Tone

*Tone* is the single most important element of your e-mail communication. That's because with e-mail, you can not rely on the tools you have with face-to-face communication, including body language and facial expressions. You don't have access to the pitch, intonation, and volume that comes with a telephone message, either. You don't even have the conventions of traditional letters—stationery color, size, shape, and even smell. (Remember sending or receiving perfumed love letters?)

Never assume your email will be interpreted exactly as you intend. Research published in *The Journal of Personality and Social Psychology* shows there is a 50 percent chance the tone of an e-mail will be misinterpreted. One example given in the article occurred when a coworker sent a congratulatory e-mail to another who was named Employee of the Month. The e-mail read this way:

*Wow. You are so awesome. I am in awe of you.*

The writer wanted to send a sincere message of approval and support, but as this reads, it could be interpreted as a sarcastic stab in the back, a "Why did you get the award and not someone else?" jab.

With your facial expression, body language, and tone of voice to support you, your message can't be so easily misinterpreted. With e-mail, you have only words on the screen. To help prevent sending an e-mail with the wrong tone, read your e-mail over with different inflections before you send it. See how each inflection affects potential meaning.

## Choose Your Words with Care

The words you choose can be formal, informal, or somewhere in between. They can be literal or figurative. They can be vague or precise, simple or complex, common or unfamiliar. For instance, you would never use slang such as *bummer, dude,* or (heaven forbid) *that sucks* in a professional email.

Since we send off e-mail so quickly and so often, the tendency is to use whatever words come to mind. You are smarter than that, so you will take the time to get the precise word you need. As American humorist and novelist Mark Twain said, "The difference between the almost right word and the right word is really a large matter—it's the difference between the lightning bug and the lightning."

## Pinpoint Your Audience

Before you choose a single word, consider your audience very carefully. Tailor the words you choose to your relationship to the recipient(s) of your e-mail. Here are some guidelines:

| Audience | Possible Tone |
| --- | --- |
| Superior, such as a supervisor or boss | deferential, respectful |
| Colleague or co-worker | friendly but professional |
| Subordinate who works for you | respectful, polite, courteous |
| A total stranger | very clear; polite and courteous |
| Readers hostile your message | neutral |
| Readers receptive to your message | friendly |

Many e-mail writers use replacements for gestures and intonation to help them convey tone. Here are some of the most common ones:

| Email Conventions | Examples |
|---|---|
| Smileys (These are on email page as a pull-down menu) | ☺   ☺   ☹ |
| Asterisks | * |
| Capital letters (All capital letters is called "Flaming" and is usually considered rude.) | Thank you A LOT. I REALLY appreciate your efforts on my behalf . |
| Creative punctuation | What is your take on this??!! |
| Font choice | I favor a very traditional font with all professional email, such as Times New Roman or Arial. However, some writers convey enthusiasm with a font such as **COMIC SANS**. |
| Whitespace (leaving blank space for emphasis) | |

If you choose to use these methods, be very sure that your audience is receptive to them. Until very recently, for instance, smileys were NEVER acceptable in business e-mails. Some companies with an informal and more relaxed power structure do use them in e-mails, but for my money, I would still avoid them in professional e-mail communication.

## Consider Not Responding

We cherish the myth that communication can solve all the world's problems, bringing peace, harmony, and smaller hip sizes. Not so. A surprising amount of time, less communication is better. This is especially true when it comes to e-mail. Here are some guidelines to make your e-mail communication more professional:

## Don't Respond When It's Not Necessary

You learned that we send a lot of e-mail . . . a whole lot. So don't add to the congestion on the information highway if you don't have to. Few things annoy people as much as unnecessary e-mail. It clogs up their in-box and wastes their time.

You are under no obligation to answer every e-mail. In most cases, people will be delighted when you don't because it saves them time. And when appropriate, tell recipients that you don't need a reply. Write something like this: "No reply necessary." It will save everyone a lot of time and win you professional goodwill.

BTW, we even have a name for unsolicited, unwanted e-mail: *spam.* Technically speaking, spam is unwanted bulk e-mail sent indiscriminately from an unknown source, but I classify any unwanted e-mail as spam.

If you receive suspicious-looking e-mail, the best thing to do is delete it unread. But if you have the Outlook Preview Pane open and you select the item even just to delete it, your machine will read the content and may be infected by any viruses embedded in it.

## Don't Copy Everyone.

Use cc (carbon copy) sparingly. Send your reply only to the people who really need it to do their job. Also, be careful not to overuse the Reply to All function. Rarely does everyone on the list need a reply.

## Forward Judiciously

Be considerate when you decide what to send on to someone. If you receive a message that had been forwarded to you from someone else, and you merely forward it to another person, the entire forwarding history of the message gets forwarded as well. Sometimes, the original message is only one sentence long, but it has been forwarded so many times, the last person to receive the forwarded message receives ten pages of forwarding history along with the actual message. Such a time-waster!

This problem becomes compounded when the message is sent to multiple recipients, because each time the message is forwarded, the list of multiple recipients for each forwarding is listed as well. Cut and paste the message to solve this problem.

### *Watch the Reply Button*

When you answer an e-mail by using the Reply button, you usually automatically copy the original e-mail message into your response. Reposting the entire initial message is appropriate if it is required for your response. However, if you require only a few lines of text from the original message in your response, delete the rest of the original message.

### *Learn How to Use the To, Cc and Bcc Functions*

When you send a message using the To: option to one person or a group, all the e-mail addresses listed in the to section of your e-mail will be listed on the e-mail of all recipients. For example, if you send one message to one hundred people at the same time, each recipient will see all 100 email addresses listed at the top of the message. The same is true when you use the cc option.

If you need to include the list of everyone getting the message, use the to or cc. If not, use the bcc. Using the bcc helps you conceal the identities of the other people receiving the message as well as saving them time. It looks far more professional than the long, unnecessary list, too.

By sending an e-mail message to someone, you have in fact allowed them to use the message however they want to. You no longer have any control over the message.

## Be Correct

It goes without saying, but I'll say it anyway: make sure your e-mails are letter-perfect. Don't be seduced into thinking that e-mail is a casual form of communication. Anything that is professional communication must be professionally written. And that means it follows the rules of standard written English.

### Proofread

Always proofread your e-mails before you send them to avoid making mistakes in grammar, usage, punctuation, and spelling. Proofreading also helps you catch problems with word usage and tone. Last but certainly not least, proofreading helps you decide if you really want to send the e-mail at all. This can often be the most important consideration of all!

### Check for Clarity

Clear writing reflects clear thinking. Muddled writing reflects muddled thinking. Your image can depend on daily informal e-mail more than on formal documents.

### Include a Signature

You would be astonished how often people forget this! It is especially important when the writer is not using a clear e-mail address. There is a quick and painless solution to this: use a basic mail signature file. This automatically attaches whatever signature information you want to your e-mails. Include some or all of the following information:

- Your name
- Your title/position in the company
- Your telephone and fax numbers
- Your e-mail address (especially appreciated if someone prints out the message)

## Glossary of E-mail Terms

E-mail jargon is being coined each day, and here are some of the most common ones.

| Term | Definition |
|------|-----------|
| bot | A piece of software that acts on behalf of and in place of a person (from roBOT) |
| bounce | A message that was returned to the sender, either because the e-mail address was incorrect or because there was a problem on the receiver's end |
| distribution list | A single e-mail address that resends e-mail to many others, allowing a discussion to continue easily among a quasi-stable group of participants (also called *E-mailing list* or *Listserv*). |
| flame | A hostile e-mail message; often written in all capital letters |
| mailbot listbot | Software that automatically replies to e-mail Software that manages distribution lists. Also called a *Listserve* or *Majordomo* (after the name of a common list server) |
| lurk | To read messages anonymously without posting |
| ping | Test to see if the other person is at his or computer and available. You would use it like this: "Drink after work? Ping me around six." |
| post | Send email to a distribution list or Usenet newsgroup |
| spam | Unsolicited e-mail sent to many people simultaneously. Spam is usually commercial, but may also be political. |

# Acknowledgments

A book is a collaborative enterprise and I have been fortunate to collaborate with the best. I'd like to thank Lisa Thornbloom, a long-time supporter as well as a great editor; Christos Peterson, the interior designer; and Randee Marullo, the copy-editor. Special thanks to Christine Zika, the Editor-in-Chief of The Literary Guild, who developed the idea for this book with me over a delicious lunch. Christine, you are a joy to work with.